The No-nonsense Credit Manual

How to repair your credit profile, manage personal debts and get the right home loan or car lease.

By: Shaun Aghili, CFP

The no-nonsense credit manual

Published by:

I.L.S. Publishing
2222 Michelson Dr. Suite 222-252
Irvine, CA 92616   USA

Copyright 1998 © by Shaun Aghili.

All rights reserved. Except as permitted under the Copyright Act of 1976, no part of this manual may be reproduced in whole or in part in any manner.

Library of Congress Cataloging-in-Publication Data

Aghili, Shaun, 1962-
    The no-nonsense credit manual: how to repair your credit profile, manage personal debts, and get the right home loan or car lease (includes the 1997 consumer law updates) / by Shaun Aghili, -- 1st ed.
    p.   cm.
    Includes index.
    ISBN: 0-9661164-2-9
    1. Consumer credit--United States. 2. Consumer credit--Law and legislation--United States. 3. Mortgage loans--United States. 4. Automobile leasing and renting--United States. I. Title.
    HG3756.U54A33 1998
    332.7'43--dc21
                                                              97-46356
                                                                   CIP

Printed in the USA by

3212 East Highway 30 • Kearney, NE 68847 • 1-800-650-7888

Consumer disclosure:

*The contents of this manual are for informational purposes ONLY. The author's intent was to better familiarize the consumer with credit reporting systems and issues. <u>**The following is NOT legal advice**</u>. It is based on the author's personal and professional experience as a financial planner and a loan officer. Use this information at your own risk. The author has no control over people requesting this information and how they intend to use it. The user of this information thus assumes full responsibility for his or her actions and decisions regarding the use of this manual.*

Preface

In 1994, there were 124 million credit card holders carrying a total balance of over $230 billion on those charge cards. That breaks down to an average of almost $3,000 per credit card, representing a whopping 41% increase from 1990! Credit cards are big business for banks who are constantly luring consumers into applying for more and more credit. The end result for many consumers is bankruptcy or at least a "spotty" credit profile due to the inability to manage their accumulated debts.

Additionally, many prospective home buyers, especially first timers, have credit issues that need to be addressed prior to qualifying for a home loan. The process of securing financing for a first house is often a complex and confusing task.

In writing this manual I want to accomplish several things. To begin, my goal is to write a simple and short manual that can be easily understood and used by just about ANYONE interested in improving his or her credit profile. It quite simply gives you the knowledge and the tools you need to know to begin improving your credit rating almost immediately. I am not an attorney and neither are most of the people that will use this information. Therefore, I felt no need to fill this book up with long pages of dry and boring legal excerpts or remotely related material. Read this manual. Absorb its contents and go to work on improving your credit rating and reducing your consumer debts.

Over the years, I have happened to come across a few reports and manuals on this subject that were advocating, in my opinion, some downright illegal methods of credit repair. I maintain that most people are above using these kinds of sleazy and unethical methods. The right way has never taken me anywhere other than my intended destination. It can and will do the very same for you, too!

This manual covers everything that you need to know about establishing, repairing and maintaining your credit profile and about handling your debts responsibly. Learn the information well and plan your strategy. Results will soon follow. Above all, learn from all your past financial mistakes.

God bless, and the best of luck.

Table of Contents

Part I: Credit basics
    Chapter 1: Covering the basics 3
    Chapter 2: Credit bureaus new "secret" weapon:
    The Fair Isaacs scoring model 9
    Chapter 3: The point scoring system 13

Part II: Establishing a track record ....
    Chapter 4: (Re-)establishing your credit profile 19

Part III: Credit repair
    Chapter 5: Credit repair basics 25
    Chapter 6: The credit repair procedure... Part 1 31
    Chapter 7: The credit repair procedure...Part 2 39

Part IV: Maintaining a good credit profile
and staying out of trouble
    Chapter 8: Cash flow management 101 49
    Chapter 9: Dealing with consumer debts:
    Financial strategies 53

Part V: Managing your biggest debt: Your mortgage
    Chapter 10: Getting approved for a home loan 61
    Chapter 11: Home loan basics 65
    Chapter 12: Deciding on a home loan program 73
    Chapter 13: Popular government and conventional
    home loan programs requiring little
    or no down payment 77
    Chapter 14: Mortgage reduction strategies...Part 1 87
    Chapter 15: Mortgage reduction strategies...Part 2 91

Part VI: Car financing
    Chapter 16: Car leases and loan programs 99

Part VII: Bits and pieces
    Chapter 17: Frequently asked questions 109
    Chapter 18: How to file a complaint 125

Part VIII: Sample dispute letters 131

Index 141

About the author 145

Part I

Credit basics

Chapter 1
Covering the basics

What are credit bureaus?

Credit bureaus, also called repositories, are central clearing houses for credit related information. There are three major credit bureaus in the United States: Experian (TRW), Transunion (TU) and Equifax (CBI/EFX). Not all creditors report to all three bureaus, although a good number of them do. Therefore, not all repositories contain the exact same information on a consumer.

Banks, insurance companies, credit unions, mortgage and car lenders, credit cards companies, as well as many other financial institutions subscribe to credit reporting companies which derive their information from one or more of the above mentioned repositories, for two reasons:

1. To ascertain the credit and payment history of an applicant.
2. To report consumer's payment history to the bureaus.

All three repositories have come up with a new credit scoring system in an attempt to further streamline the creditor's loan approval process. Since credit reporting is a highly automated process, many files do contain inaccurate, obsolete or misleading information without the consumer's knowledge. This in turn also affects a consumer's credit scores. Therefore, a yearly credit check up to ensure that your credit files are accurate is highly recommended.

A primer on federal laws on credit and debt collection:

The Truth in Lending Act requires all credit grantors to provide you with appropriate disclosure information. These include the annual percentage rate (APR), costs and terms, payments, prepayment penalties and all other relevant information.

The Equal Credit Opportunity Act prohibits a lender or creditor to discriminate against a credit applicant because of age, sex, marital status, race, color, religion, national origin, receipt of any public aid or any exercise of legal rights.

The Fair Credit Reporting Act is designed to help consumers correct mistakes on their credit files. This law also requires that all credit files be kept confidential.

The Fair Credit Billing Act sets up a procedure for promptly correcting errors on a credit account in order to prevent any damage to your credit while an account is being disputed for accuracy between the consumer and the credit grantor.

The Consumer Leasing Act requires disclosure of information to help you compare costs and terms between leasing plans. It also requires that leasing companies reveal facts that can help the consumer compare the cost and terms of leasing versus buying on credit or with cash.

The Fair Debt Collection Practices Act regulates people and firms that are in the bill collection business. It prohibits them from performing abusive collection practices and allows consumers to dispute a debt and halt unreasonable collection activities.

What is in a credit report?

A credit file is basically composed of the following parts:

Consumer identification information: Credit bureaus identify consumers by their complete name, social security number, date of birth and current address. A previous address is also required if the consumer has been residing at his or her current address for less than two years. *It is therefore very important to supply all of the above mentioned information wherever you request your credit file from TRW, Transunion or Equifax.*

Credit history: The name and account number of each subscriber is listed, along with the consumer's payment history. Each **trade line** usually shows when the account was opened, whether it is an individual or joint account, its maximum limit, its current limit, its required payment as well as how many times a consumer was 30, 60, or 90 days late on the trade. This section may also contain information about consumer disputes, charge-offs and collection accounts. *Credit bureaus can keep any derogatory credit information on a consumer's file for up to seven years.*

Public records: This section of the report shows any tax liens, bankruptcies, judgements, and other public courthouse records. *Bankruptcies stay on record for ten years.* We will discuss how to remove or dispute inaccurate or outdated information in your credit history or public records in detail later.

Credit inquiries: Every time a subscriber runs a credit report on a consumer, the computer at the credit repository records an inquiry. This inquiry remains on a consumer's record for about 18 months. It is against the law for anyone to run your credit without your consent, which must usually be given in writing. These inquiries are of interest to creditors since it gives them an idea about the applicant's recent credit dealings. An excessive amount of inquiries is considered a "red light" for creditors. What is considered excessive? In the mortgage lending business, anything more than an inquiry or two every ninety days constitutes a "red light."

Consumer tip: Car dealers are notorious about running your credit every time you visit a showroom and sit down to discuss financing. You need to be very careful about this issue when car buying. Order a credit report from all three major repositories and keep the copies with you when you visit a showroom. Do not let a dealer run a credit report unless you have made up your mind on a particular model and have negotiated a fair price for it. Allow them to run their own report once the deal is about to be finalized.

Consumer statements: Not many people are aware of the fact that they have the legal right to put on their credit report a statement of up to 100 words regarding any items they wish to explain or clarify. As you will soon find out, this technique is very powerful if used in conjunction with other procedures in helping you to improve your credit rating.

How to obtain your credit reports directly from the credit bureaus:

Experian (TRW): P.O. Box 949
Allen, TX 75013
(800) 643-3334
www.experian.com

You can obtain one FREE report a year by writing to:

TRW Complimentary Report
P. O. Box 2350
Chatsworth, CA 91313

Transunion (TU): P.O. Box 390
Springfield, PA 19064
(800) 916-8800
$8.00/report
www.tuc.com

Equifax (CBI/EFX): P.O. Box 740241
Atlanta, GA 30374
(800) 685-1111
One FREE report a year.
www.equifax.com/consumer.html

Important note: If you have been denied credit within the past 30 days, based on the information derived from any of the above bureaus, you can request a FREE copy of your credit profile from that repository. Also, use these same addresses for all other correspondence with the bureaus.

Chapter 2
Credit bureau's new "secret" weapon: The Fair Isaacs scoring model

The new credit bureau scores were designed for the mortgage industry a few short years ago by a San Rafael, CA-based company called Fair, Isaac & Co. The Fair, Isaacs scoring model is a vast improvement over the other more primitive scoring models in use. It is designed to provide a statistical estimate of a loan's future performance by using actual loan performances, as observed in samples of over 750,000 consumers from the credit bureau's databases to assign a credit risk score to an individual credit file.

All three repositories use the same Fair, Isaacs risk scoring model, but each bureau has a different name for it.

TRW/Experian: FICA
Transunion: EMPIRICA
CBI/EFX: BEACON

Information which is predictive of future credit risk includes:

Previous credit performance: This includes late payments, collection and charge-off accounts, tax liens, bankruptcies, etc... The Fair, Isaacs risk model takes into consideration the ENTIRE history of the consumer's credit file, not just the past year or two.

Current level of indebtedness: If most of your credit cards are charged up to the hilt, that will have a rather negative effect on your credit scores even if you have a clean payment history. That is one of the many reasons you should pay off or pay your balances down as quickly as possible.

Excessive inquiries: Every time you apply for credit, an inquiry is made to your credit file. Inquiries are covered in more detail later. For now, keep in mind that they do impact your credit scores negatively.

Amount of time credit has been in use: Consumers with long-term, clean credit histories tend to have higher scores than the ones with a more recent track record.

Type of credit used: High loan amounts such as mortgages that are always paid on time tend to improve a consumer's credit score in a major way. Lower limit accounts tend to have a lesser impact.

Does Fair, Isaac's scoring take income into consideration?

No! Income, race, gender, religion, national origin, marital status or the fact that an individual is receiving public assistance has no bearing whatsoever on this credit score model. However, income will be taken into consideration during most loan or credit approval processes.

What is a good credit score?

An increasing number of home lenders are requiring a minimum FICA score of at least 620. Some lenders and other creditors have higher requirements. Generally, credit scores in the 660 and above range are considered good. The reason I call the Fair, Isaacs risk model a "secret" weapon is that most lenders and creditors are not likely to disclose these credit scores to you, and you will not see these numbers on any credit reports you order directly from the bureaus. This system is still new and under scrutiny. It was conceived for lenders and creditors to be used as an internal tool only.

Where do these magic numbers come from?

Based on a statistical study done by the Federal National Mortgage Corporation (Fannie Mae) from April of 1994 to April of 1996, borrowers with a FICA score of 660 or more had the lowest rate of foreclosure and were considered "vanilla" loans. Those with a score of 620 to 659 were about three times more likely to go to default, and were labeled as "gray area" loans. Finally, borrowers with a score of less than 620 were about EIGHT times more likely to default on a mortgage than the "vanilla" loan category clients.

Chapter 3
The point scoring system

This system has been in use for credit card approvals for a number of years now. It is being very gradually adapted on a much more sophisticated level by a few major home loan investors. The idea here is to assign points to each section of an application and then tally the scores to arrive at a final lending decision. A point scoring system may very well also take credit scores (FICO, BEACON or EMPIRICA) into consideration. Credit card applications are most often reviewed and graded by a computer point scoring system. The following is a hypothetical example of such a system used by a credit card company or bank to grant credit.

Employment/current position held for:
Less than one year: -1 point
1 to 2 years: 2 points
More than 2 but less than 4 years: 2 points
More than 4 years: 3 points

Length of current residence:
Less than one year: 0 points
More than 1 year: 1 point
More than 2 years: 2 points
More than 3 years: 3 points

Gross monthly income:
Less than $1,000: -2 points
$1,001 to $1,999: 1 point
Over $2,000: 2 points

Over $3,000: 3 points
Over $4,500: 4 points

Savings account:
Yes: 1 point
No: 0 points

Checking accounts:
Yes: 1 point
No: -2 points

Current living arrangement:
Lives with parents: 0 points
Renting: 1 point
Homeowner: 2 points

Current lines of credit:
None: - 3 points
1-2: 1 point
3-5: 2 points
More than five: 3 points

Current/Previous loan or account at this bank:
No previous account history: 0 points
Previous account had more than one late payment: -3 points
Previous account has been paid in full with no lates: 3 points

Credit derogatories in the past two years:
None: 3 points
1-2: -2 points
3-4: -4 points
More than 4: -5 points

Scoring system:
16-20: Very good credit risk. Automatic approval.
12-15: Reasonable risk. Approval subject to supervisor's review and approval.
Less than 12: Automatic rejection.

Further automation through perfecting point scoring systems and credit risk models will be the future of the lending industry. You are now familiar with some of the tools that home lenders and credit card companies use to evaluate your credit application.

Part II

Establishing a track record

Chapter 4
(Re-)establishing your credit profile

Whether you are a recent college graduate trying to build your credit profile or you have filed bankruptcy (B/K) a couple of years ago and are interested in re-establishing your credit, you will greatly benefit from the suggestions in this section. In today's society it is very difficult to function without a credit profile, although as a loan officer I have always maintained that NO CREDIT IS GOOD CREDIT!

Establishing a track record

If you are a recent graduate or have never had credit before, there are several other ways to establish credit besides obtaining a secured credit card. I suggest them for you as easy and fast ways to obtain credit. Other ways to establish credit include:

1. **Have a parent or spouse with good credit add you on to one of her accounts as an additional card holder.** The caveat here is if that person ever becomes delinquent on that debt obligation or slow pays the account, it will also be reflected on your credit file as well. So be careful!

2. **Apply for a gas card or a department store card first.** Since many start you off with a fairly small line of credit, they are often more willing to extend credit to someone with no credit background. These include cards such as EXXON, SHELL, J.C. PENNEY, etc...

3. **Apply for a student credit card.** Companies like American Express or Bank of America will give unsecured credit cards with a fairly low limit to college students just starting out. If you are a senior in college about to graduate or a recent graduate, give this a try.

4. **Cross Country Bank,** (800) 262-3610, will issue an unsecured credit card. They charge a $100 application fee and start you out with a credit limit of $350.00.

Re-establishing credit after a bankruptcy

If you have filed a Chapter 7 bankruptcy (B/K) that has been discharged, you owe it to yourself to get back on your feet as soon as possible since re-establishing credit is a task that may take you several years. Your first line of attack is to order a copy of your credit report from all three credit bureaus several months after the discharge of your B/K. You want to make sure that all the accounts dismissed under your B/K have been correctly identified as *"Dismissed under bankruptcy."* If there are errors in your report or it has not been correctly updated, then you need to write to the credit bureau and request a correction. Additionally, make sure your B/K is also listed as *"discharged"* under the public record section of your report.

****
YOU CANNOT AFFORD TO HAVE ANY DEROGATORY CREDIT INFORMATION ON YOUR CREDIT FILE FOLLOWING A BANKRUPTCY IF YOU ARE INTERESTED IN RE-ESTABLISHING YOUR CREDIT!
****

If the reason for the bankruptcy was due to your inability to manage debt, you must reevaluate your spending habits and make a commitment not to get yourself into a financial predicament ever again! Bankruptcy is an opportunity for many people to get a new start in life. It is NOT an easy way out of getting out of paying your creditors.

Your best bet to re-establish credit after a B/K is to apply for a secured credit card. Each bank has a different eligibility policy. Make sure you find out about their guidelines regarding B/K by calling them first. A secured credit card is a VISA or MASTERCARD that requires a collateral savings account deposit often equivalent to your line of credit. Most require a $500 deposit while a few banks have lower initial deposit requirements.

For a list of secured credit cards write to:
        Bankcard Holders of America
        524 Branch Drive
        Salem, VA 24153
        (540)389-5445
        $4.00 fee per list

Keep in mind that you CANNOT use your initial collateral deposit to pay off your secured credit card. These cards are a way to establish a timely track record. I suggest you try to pay off your full amount due each month to save on finance charges and to keep your available credit intact for emergencies. People with a discharged B/K ought to start out with one or two secured credit cards, and establish a track record of two years before trying to apply for unsecured credit.

Consumer tip: Many secured credit card issuers are reporting these entries as "secured debt" to the credit bureaus. Enroll in a secured credit card program that reports the card just like a regular Visa or Mastercard. It looks much better on your credit file! Call the issuer's customer service number and ask them if they report the card as a secured debt or the same way as a regular unsecured charge card.

Part III

Credit repair

Chapter 5
Credit repair basics

My personal experience with two credit repair companies:

There are a number of credit repair companies that advertise *"guaranteed"* results. I have seen and heard of fees as low as $250.00 to over $1,000. The very idea for this manual is to allow **YOU** to do a lot less expensively and often better and quicker what these credit repair people promise to do. Beginning in the early part of 1996, new laws were passed to protect the public against the sometimes unscrupulous business practices of these companies. This will soon put all of these credit repair clinics out of business. While I don't condemn every organization involved in credit repair, I would like to share my personal experience dealing with a couple of them.

A little over ten years ago, I came out of a business endeavor with my brother with heavy debts and a damaged credit profile. I was about ten thousand dollars in debt, with several delinquent accounts. After consulting with an attorney about filing bankruptcy, I decided not to listen to her advice because it seemed to me that she was more interested in her $500 bankruptcy fee than in giving me decent legal advice. I decided to go at it myself. I saw an ad for *The Consumer Counseling Service* and called up for an appointment. Today, C.C.C.S. is a non-profit organization with local chapters in over 800 cities. They helped me to set up a repayment plan and confiscated all my credit cards. I remained on their plan for almost three years and managed to pay off a major portion of my credit card debts.

One day, I saw an ad for one of these credit repair places and made an appointment to see a counselor. We discussed my situation, and he told me that they needed an initial "down payment" of $250.00 to get me started. All along, my gut feeling was telling me something was fishy about this operation, but since I couldn't put my finger on anything, I dismissed it as paranoia. Anyway, they told me they would send out my first set of dispute letters in about two weeks.

Two weeks came and went— but no dispute letters! I called, but the phone was disconnected! I went in person to see what was going on, only to find out that they were no longer in business. According to the building manager, an FBI agent was also looking for them! I felt like such a fool. Here I was out $250 dollars and was taken by a bunch of con artists. Several months passed. Another one of these credit miracle companies was spending a small fortune on TV advertising and was presenting itself as a division of a law office. I was determined to clean up my credit. I called and they sent in a pushy salesman that drilled me for over an hour to get a signed contract and a deposit for $200. I wasn't about to make the same mistake twice. I got rid of the guy and spent the next week calling the Better Business Bureau, the district attorney's office and several other places trying to check these guys out. I couldn't find anything suspicious on them, so I went to their office unannounced and talked to their sales manager. It was a rather big operation and they seemed to be doing a lot of business. I signed a bunch of papers and paid over $850 during the next year only to have ONE collection account removed from my report! They stopped sending me dispute letters to sign and mail to my creditors after they got all their money. By this time, I was leaving Houston for L.A. and therefore was not really able to do much else to get them to either refund my money or do a better job at cleaning up my credit profile.

By the time I came to California, I had read and learned enough about credit repair that I started writing my own dispute letters. I taught myself how to negotiate charge-off accounts with creditors, how to re-establish my credit and how to keep myself from getting into trouble again.

The new 1997 Credit Repair Organization Act

New legislation finally went into effect in April of 1997 that will put most unscrupulous credit repair outfits out of business. It stipulates that credit repair companies can no longer accept payments until services are fully rendered.

Additionally, all organizations involved in credit repair must give prospective clients a written contract. This contract outlines all payments and terms as well as any guarantees of performance and gives an estimate of how long it will take them to provide the service in full. A written disclosure explaining the customer's legal rights regarding their credit history must also be provided to the consumer. Despite all these new safeguards, you can always do as good a job for a lot less money yourself as long as you learn the proper procedure.

What is my credit repair approach capable of doing for YOU?

What I provide you here is a LEGAL and ETHICAL way to improve your credit profile that is derived mainly from personal experience. **IT IS NOT A GUARANTEED SYS-**

<u>TEM</u> and I am certainly not going to give you legal advice. I am simply going to show you how to improve your credit rating YOURSELF without getting ripped off, like I was. **This system takes organization, persistence and time.** How long will it take? It is difficult to tell. It may take as little as 30 to 60 days, or as long as several years. How effective is it? I think it is pretty darned effective, although there are no guarantees since each situation is different.

I have seen manuals advocating unethical techniques such as creating alternate credit files which try to trick credit bureaus. In my opinion, people who use these techniques or advocate them ought to be prosecuted and put behind bars! Give the system outlined for you here a decent chance and I am confident you will be impressed with the results.

I suggest that you study this section in the following manner:

1. *Read over the entire section once, to get a basic understanding of the procedure.*
2. *Re-read the entire section a second time, this time highlighting and making notes for yourself as you go along. You'll need to outline a personal strategy for yourself since each situation is different. Therefore, you really need to use your deductive reasoning abilities and answer a lot of your own questions after you absorb this material. Credit repair is not a difficult procedure at all, once you understand its basics.*

A few very important key points before we begin:

I encourage you to add your personal touch to the sample letters at the end of this manual, as long as you don't deviate from their basic outline. If your handwriting is anything like mine, I suggest you type these letters on your word processor, otherwise feel free to hand write them if you wish. **Make sure your letters** are legible. *You must remain organized at all times. Make up a "credit" file on yourself and keep a copy of all of your dispute letters and other correspondence. You must keep accurate notes on when you mailed your dispute letters as well as any telephone conversations with creditors or credit bureaus. Always get the full name of the person you talk to. All dispute letters must be sent via CERTIFIED, RETURN RECEIPT MAIL. Above all, always remain pleasant and polite when dealing with creditors or credit bureaus. You'll get much better results that way!*

Your legal rights under the Fair Credit Reporting Act

You have the right:

1. To be provided information about the nature and source of the information collected about you by a credit bureau.

2. To obtain this information at no charge, provided you have been denied credit, insurance or employment, within 30 days. (Keep in mind that you must contact the bureau whose information was used to decline your request.)

3. To be able to take anyone of your choosing with you when visiting a credit bureau.

4. To be told who has received a credit report on you within the past six months or the past two years if the report was furnished for employment purposes.

5. To have incorrect, incomplete or obsolete information reinvestigated, and if found inaccurate or unverified, to have such information deleted permanently from your file.

6. To have the right to have a consumer statement added on to your credit report.

7. To have your credit report withheld from anyone who does not have a legitimate business need for the information.

8. To sue a company for damages arising from illegal or neglectful use of your credit information.

9. To be notified if a company is requesting a consumer report, and to be informed of its nature and the scope of investigation.

10. To have negative information removed from your report after seven years, except for bankruptcies which will stay in your file for ten years.

Chapter 6
The credit repair procedure (Part I)

New regulations enacted in late 1997 under the federal Fair Credit Reporting Act, have given consumers more power than ever to repair their own credit profiles. Credit bureaus are now required more than simply contact a creditor following the receipt of a dispute letter to verify the accuracy of any items on a credit file.

Repositories must now:
1. Contact the creditor within five days of receiving your dispute letter.
2. Complete an investigation within 30 days of the receipt of your complaint.
3. Review all information you have supplied.
4. Adopt procedures to keep deleted information from reappearing.
5. Provide you with the results of its investigation within five days of completion.

Additionally all creditors reporting to credit bureaus must:
1. Refrain from ignoring information that contradicts what they have on file.
2. Provide credit bureaus with correct and updated information once they learn that the previous information on file was erroneous.

Your suggested game plan:

Obtain a copy of your credit report from TRW, EFX and TU: Refer to the first section of this course if you are still unclear about how to order these reports. Use the sample request letter #1 as your guide.

Once you receive the reports, you need to analyze the information: Up until a few years ago, credit reports were compiled in a rather consumer unfriendly manner. Fortunately, credit bureaus have made some improvements in this area, so reading a credit report requested directly from any of the major credit bureaus is no longer a very difficult task. It is therefore not necessary to spend any time going into details about how to read these reports. You want to go over your report with a pencil and a highlighter and check the following areas:

Personal identification information: First name, last name, middle initial, Social Security number, current address... Are they all correct? There may also be additional information about your employment, marital status, name of spouse, and so on. Make notes of any and all inaccurate information. *Keep in mind that if your Social Security number is mistyped, you need to send the bureau a copy of your S.S. card. Likewise, a correction of your date of birth, the spelling of your name or current address requires you to send them a copy of your driver's license.*

Collection and charge-off accounts: Here is a brief explanation of what these accounts signify. If you have defaulted on an account, it will very likely be referred to the creditor's collection department. They will try to bring the account up to date or to settle it by writing you letters and/or calling you. If they are not successful in their collection efforts, sooner or later the creditor will write off the account as an uncollectible debt on its books, thus the term "charge-off." They may then refer or sell the note at a discount to other outside collection agencies who will then try to collect from you. **Collection and charge-off accounts are the easiest entries to remove from your credit profile, so you want to handle them first.** You will accomplish this in two steps: First, you will ask the bureau to verify that the collection account REALLY does belong to you. Second, if the account gets verified as accurate, you will contact the creditor and negotiate a discounted pay off, along with a written agreement from the collection company that they will remove the collection or "charge-off" entry from your credit profile once it is paid in full.

I must also point out a potential caveat in trying to dispute charge-offs and collection accounts. It is possible that you could instigate a new wave of collection letters in trying to dispute a certain charge-off/collection entry. As you will shortly see, this is not necessarily a bad thing. I'll show you how to even turn it into your advantage. However, the point is this: Even though you need to do as good a job as possible the first time around, **be careful!** *If you have a lot of large balance collection/charge-off accounts, it is prudent to split them up into several batches and dispute them at regular three or four months intervals.*

Not quite clear?
Let me clarify the point through an example.

Let's say I get my credit reports back and find out I have the following collection/charge-off accounts (among other things).

1. *A Pacific Bell collection account for $75.00 that is three years old reported on TRW & EFX.*

2. *A medical collection account for $125.00 that is four years old reported on TRW & TU.*

3. A charge-off account on an old VISA card with an outstanding balance of $1200.00 that is three years old reported on TRW, EFX and TU.

4. A charge-off account on American Express for $750.00 that is four years old reported on TRW, TU & EFX.

This is going to be my strategy:

In my first letter, I will dispute the PAC BELL, the medical collection and the VISA account with the proper credit bureaus. Let's assume that thirty days later I get updated reports from the bureaus and I find out that the PAC BELL collection is still on TRW (but no longer on EFX). The medical collection is wiped out from all three credit reports, and the VISA card is still on all three repositories. A week later, I start getting collection letters from VISA.

What happened here?

First of all, TRW was able to verify my collection account with PAC BELL. However EFX was not as lucky, so they had to delete it from my EFX report! Next, the medical collection company did not verify that the charge-off was mine to either TRW or TU —it happens all the time!— so the entry was deleted from both repositories. Lastly, the bank that issued the VISA card not only verified the debt as belonging to me, but since they received this inquiry from all three bureaus, they figured that this is a good time to start their collection efforts again! Now is this bad? Not necessarily!

Here is what I'll do next:

I will contact PAC BELL by mail and offer a settlement of $50.00, with one condition: They must provide me IN

WRITING with a statement that they will remove the collection account from ALL the credit bureaus they reported it to within thirty days after my negotiated payment. They may accept that, or they may reply saying that they will remove it only if I pay the full amount. I figure that is a fair proposal, so I write back to them and accept their counter offer. **However, I WILL NOT pay the $75.00 until I have a WRITTEN agreement from PAC BELL stating they will remove the account from my credit reports.** Why? Very simple reason. Creditors are not very motivated to help you out AFTER they get their money! You will have ten times more leverage this way. After all, it is a win-win situation... Isn't it?

Now, I need to take care of the VISA situation. I noticed that these VISA folks are really nice! They sent me a settlement proposal offering to settle the $1,200.00 overdue account for a onetime payment of $900, which is a seventy-five cents on the dollar settlement of the debt. Interesting! I write back to them, thanking them for their generosity and offer the following: Three consecutive $200.00 monthly payments to FULLY settle the account **ONLY IF THEY PUT IN WRITING THAT THEY WILL REMOVE THE COLLECTION ACCOUNT FROM MY CREDIT FILES NO LATER THAN THIRTY DAYS FOLLOWING FULL SETTLEMENT OF MY DEBT!** Guess what? They write back accepting my offer! So I get to settle my debt at fifty cents on the dollar, **AND** have it removed for good from my credit profile.

Now I wait about four months before attacking the last collection account.

Remember, your file gets marked every time your credit file gets investigated. You don't want excessive notes on your credit files. Why did I choose to do it this way versus disputing all four collections at once? I did not want to get in a situation where I get collection letters from three or four creditors at once! I handled the little stuff first, along with one major account. I took care of them first before moving on to my other bigger collection account. If necessary, I could follow the same procedure with my American Express collection account without straining myself financially.

DO NOT AGREE TO A PAYMENT TERM YOU CANNOT ADHERE TO! *For one thing, you are going to lose complete credibility with the creditor and may never be given a second chance. But most important, every time you start out a payment plan on an old account, you also reactivate the statute of limitations on that debt. Without getting too technical, it means that the creditor can continue to show your old debt as delinquent for another seven years and the creditor may be in a much better position to take you to court to collect. Call the shots and stick with your word. Be fair to the creditor and to yourself.*

What happens if the creditor is not interested in cooperating?

This can happen. You'll need to call them by phone and get them to start negotiating. You can get their phone number from the bureau(s) where they reported the collection account(s). Get them to commit to you that they will remove the collection accounts from your credit reports even if you have to pay them in full. Work out a realistic payment schedule. If you follow my strategies, you ought to be able to clean up most, if not all, your collection accounts. I have helped many borrowers with this strategy to remove ALL their collection accounts. You simply need to be persistent and willing to work at it.

Settling a debt for less than the original owed:

Beware of hidden tax traps! A creditor that agrees to settle a debt for less than the amount owed is required by the IRS to send you a Form 1099 at the end of the tax year if the debt forgiven is $600 or more. Let's say you had a $1700.00 unpaid (open) collection account. You talked the creditor into settling for four payments of $250.00. In essence the creditor "forgave" you for $700.00 of the amount due. They may send you a 1099 form for $700.00 for that tax year, and you are required to report that $700.00 as income on your tax returns.

In practice, I have noticed that a lot of charge-off accounts are referred or sold to outside collection companies. When you settle with these collection entities, they sometimes won't send you a 1099 form. But you can never tell if they will or not. That is another reason I suggest working on your open collection and charge-offs accounts in batches. **It is a very good idea to seek the advice of your tax preparer if you have many large charge-off accounts that you are planning to settle as you clean up your credit profile.** You may need to split them up over a few tax years in order to avoid owing the IRS more taxes than you anticipated.

Chapter 7
The credit repair procedure (Part II)

Public records: Very often, this section of the report contains old information. For example, it may show your paid-off tax liens or bankruptcy as *"status unknown"* versus *"released"* (tax liens) or *"discharged"* (B/K). There could be some duplications as well. You could dispute these public records, but they are a lot easier to verify than a collection account. Your best bet is to pay off your judgement or tax liens and to make sure they are marked as "paid" or "released." Unfortunately, bankruptcies remain on your credit file for ten years.

Revolving and installment accounts derogatories (derogs): The difference between a revolving and an installment account is as follows. Revolving accounts have a maximum credit limit with varying balances and payment dues every month. Examples include: VISA, AMEX gas cards, Sears, etc... Installment accounts have a decreasing balance and fixed payments every month. Examples of these are car payments, second mortgages, etc... **They are rated as the number of times they have been 30, 60 and 90 days late. Obviously, a perfect rating shows ZERO late payments.**

In evaluating these types of accounts you want to check for the following:

1. **Are there any accounts on the report that are NOT yours?** Don't be surprised to find accounts that may not

belong to you. They need to be disputed as "not belonging to you." See sample dispute letters at the end of this manual.

2. **Do you agree with the credit rating of the account?** Let's say you have a Sears account that is rated as two times sixty day late and three times ninety days late. You could dispute the accuracy of this rating. See sample letters.

Remember that the law stipulates that if an entry is not 100% accurate and verifiable it must be deleted. However 100% is very often a difficult goal to reach, especially when it comes to verifying credit information. If you dig deep enough, you may very well find something in that entry that is not 100% accurate. This will then constitute the nucleus of your dispute letter. You must additionally insist on WRITTEN and VERIFIABLE proof that the entry is accurate. For example:

- Are you NOT a co-signer on the account?
- Is the account number correct?
- Are the terms, high limit, the opening date, or the current status of the entry correct?
- Were you billed the wrong amount?
- Did you withhold payment due to a dispute or an unauthorized charge to the card?
- Was your payment credited to the right account?
- Did you ever return part of the order?
- Was the account really late as shown? Was it only late 15 or 20 days, and not 30?

Once you find at least one reason the entry is not accurate, then you have a right to request an investigation. It is possible that disputing these late entries may not improve their ratings on the first try. In this case, you will need to send a second (or possibly a third or fourth) dispute letter demanding that the bureau thoroughly investigate the matter.

Consumer statements: If all else fails, you can always add a brief consumer statement next to the account. This is only effective if you have one (or two at the most) accounts that have derogatory ratings. As a loan officer, I will tell you that lenders and other creditors are not interested in your sob stories. However, if you do decide to add a consumer statement, follow these guidelines:

1. Be brief and to the point: Although you can take up to 100 words to explain your position, do it with as few words as possible.

2. Your reason for late payments needs to be due to circumstances beyond your control. A sudden layoff or sickness in the family, an unexpected long trip, faulty bank drafts, etc...

3. It also helps if you conclude your statement by explaining how this was an isolated situation and not likely to ever happen again.

Let me reiterate: This is only effective if used for one or two accounts. If you don't like to pay your bills on time, then you have to work on that. You must re-evaluate your financial habits if you are interested in improving your credit profile!

Credit inquiries: As mentioned before, an excessive number of inquiries is a red light for most lenders or creditors. In most states, inquiries stay on your report for about 18 months, but most creditors look at your inquiry activity for the past ninety days. It is really not necessary to use any of the dispute methods to remove inquiries. Just keep in mind that most lenders and creditors look only at inquiries within the past ninety days of a loan application. Morale of the story? Don't go crazy applying for credit! Space out your applications for credit wisely for optimum results.

Dealing with Government Student Loans

Government student loans (GSLs) are really strange animals! Many individuals who have defaulted on GSLs have found out that they are now facing not only possible litigation but collection fees and late penalties that are often not even dischargeable under a Chapter 7 bankruptcy! I am personally aware of a few cases where the late penalty charges and interest had inflated the loan balance to more than double its original balance.

Once in default, most debtor obligations are subject to a statute of limitation which varies from state to state. Unfortunately there is no statute of limitation on GSLs, which means you can be sued and taken to court, no matter how old the loan is. To discharge a GSL under a Chapter 7 bankruptcy is a very difficult task that does not happen too often. The debt must be at least seven years old and you must convince the bankruptcy judge that you will undergo EXTREME and undue hardship if you are ordered to repay the loan (Good luck!).

Preventive measures: Your best defense

If you are currently behind on your payments or about to default on a GSL, your best bet is to contact the loan holder immediately and discuss any of the following alternatives:

Deferment: A deferment puts your payments on hold while stopping the interest accumulation clock on the account. It is only a viable alternative to discuss if you are returning back to school to pursue another degree. The loan holder may also grant you a deferment on the loan if you can prove sudden unemployment or disability.

Forbearance: If you can't qualify for a deferment, this is may be your next best bet. A forbearance allows you to either reduce or put your monthly payments on hold for the short term. Unlike a deferment, interest will continue to accrue on your loan. Once again, you must convince the loan holder why you deserve to be considered for forbearance.

Graduated or income based repayment: As the names imply, these payment alternatives allow you to reduce your regular monthly payments and give you a chance to keep up. The caveat here is that if you pick a payment amount that is too low to even cover the interest portion, you will eventually end up with an increasing loan balance in a few years! The good news is that you may be allowed as much as five more years to pay off your debts. Just work out a reasonable and yet adequate monthly payment so that you can pay the obligation off within the allowed term.

Loan consolidation: If you have several student loans, you may want to look at consolidating all of them into one, preferably lower-interest loan. The idea here is the same as using an equity line of credit on your house to pay off all your credit card debts. Due to the complexity of servicing federal student loans, only a handful of lenders offer consolidation programs.

Here is how to contact the major ones:

Sallie Mae	(800) 524-9100
USA Group	(800) 382-4506
Citibank	(800) 967-2400
Federal Direct Consolidation Loan Information Center	(800) 557-7392

You can also call the Secretary of Education borrower services at (800) 848-0979 or visit their web site at www.ed.gov/ for more information.

GSL Post-default credit repair strategy

Reinstatement and rehabilitation: The idea here is to contact your loan servicer and reinstate your account. Feel free to negotiate a graduated or income-based payment schedule, if necessary. Since you will not be able to settle the debt any time soon, your account is only considered reinstated after you make at least 6 voluntary, on time payments. Once you make at least 12 on time payments, your account will actually be considered rehabilitated. After about 12 or more months, you can contact the loan holder and/or the credit bureaus to make sure your account is being rated as "current" and "paid on time."

If you need further information about fixing your defaulted student loan, contact:

Coalition for Student Loan Reform
1875 Connecticut Ave, N.W.
Washington, D. C. 20009
(202) 328-6109
www.cslr.com

Credit repair is a game of planning, perseverance and clever negotiation. You have to know your rights and have an idea of what you can and cannot do, and then go to work. If your intentions are honorable and you genuinely want to make good on your defaulted financial obligations, you will win in the long run. Plan your work and work your plan, and as said before be fair to yourself and to your creditor. In the end you will come out victorious!

Part IV

Maintaining a good credit profile and staying out of trouble

Chapter 8
Cash flow management 101

An inability to save is very often the real culprit to excessive personal debts. In 1995, total personal income in the United States amounted to over 6 billion dollars. Sadly, Americans saved less than 4.5% of their personal income, an average not only well below most other European countries and Japan, but also about half of what it used to be in 1980. **The road to financial prosperity can start if you implement 3 basic principles and live by them from now on!**

Eliminate wasteful daily spending:

In my opinion, budgeting is like dieting. It seldom works because its effects are only short term. The only true way to lose weight and to keep it off is to change your attitude toward food. In other words, you must learn to look at food as nourishment and not as a means of emotional gratification. The same is true with money. You need to change your attitude about spending it. The easiest way is to evaluate your spending habits every couple of months and to cut out all the waste.

Here's what you need to do: Keep a log of all your spending for a month. You don't need to record every quarter, but be as accurate as possible. At the end of this month, spend 30 minutes looking at all your expenses and try to pick any expenses you could have avoided if you really wanted to.

Examples of expense-related activities that can reduce or eliminate parts of your budget include:

Have coffee and cereal at home in the morning rather than stopping by the local pastry shop.
Carry your lunch to work on most days.
Share a ride rather than drive to work.
Reduce lottery ticket purchases to one a week, or eliminate altogether.
Use coupons when grocery shopping.
Reduce restaurant dining to only twice a month.
Time your clothes shopping with big sales, or shop at discount stores.
Give up or reduce expensive hobbies or habits—quit smoking!
Buy cars that make better economic sense.
If possible, move closer to your workplace to shorten your commute.
Consider getting a roommate to share expenses.
Hold a garage sale to get rid of seldom used items and use the proceeds to pay down your credit cards.
Pay off your credit card balances at the end of each month to avoid finance interest charges.
Consolidate bank accounts to avoid unnecessary charges.
Avoid taking cash from teller machines that charge you up to $1.00 per transaction.
Pay all bills on time to avoid late charges.
Compare prices when shopping by computer or T.V.
Avoid upgrading to what is simply "new and improved" but not "necessary."
Cancel T.V. cable channels you rarely watch.
Refinance your mortgage to lower your payments.
Refinance your high-interest credit cards into a lower-interest card.
Review your insurance plans to find out if you can get a similar coverage for less cost.

Cancel gold cards and cards you rarely use but for which you are charged a yearly renewal fee.
Cancel gym memberships you don't use.
Cancel speculative investments you have lost money in.
Quit upgrading your car every year or so.
Cut excessive use of cellular phones. If your mobile phone bill is over $70.00 a month and your employer does not reimburse you, get a beeper and ask people to page you instead of calling you. As a matter of fact, don't give out your mobile phone number. Also minimize the use of your phone by avoiding all calls that are not urgent.

When I did this exercise for my own benefit, I was able to cut my monthly "garbage" expenses by over $140.00 a month. This amounts to $1,680.00 a year that I ended up putting in my IRA account!

Over 20 years, assuming a modest 8% yearly return on my continuing annual contributions, I'll have an additional $90,000 saved for my retirement!

Pay yourself first:

Think about this for a second. You go to work everyday to earn a living, but what happens to your paycheck?

It gets deposited into your checking account to pay the landlord or your mortgage lender, the car leasing company, the credit card company, the grocer, the dry cleaner, the video store, etc., etc.

But the secret to always having money in the bank is to ALWAYS PAY YOURSELF FIRST!

It's that easy! Next time you get a paycheck, take out 10% from the top, and put it in your savings account

BEFORE you pay anyone else. Better yet, set up an automatic debit on your checking account so that 10% of each paycheck gets deposited into your savings or money market account.

I know from personal experience that it is more easily said than done, but you need to do it. The sooner you start, the better off you will be.

Live with as little debt as possible:

Although some debt may be inevitable (car, student or mortgage loans) as suggested before, you should try to keep your debts to a minimum. If you currently have more than a couple thousand dollars in credit card debt, use your 10% savings system in the following way:

1) Save the equivalent of one month's reserve for basic living expenses.
2) Direct your 10% savings and any other excess savings toward paying off ALL your revolving debts.
3) Continue building your emergency fund to three months.
4) Once your credit card debts are paid off and your emergency fund is up to par, you may then start a regular investment program.

The reasoning for this is that you need to pay off non-tax deductible and high interest debt first, before you beef up your savings. It doesn't make sense to earn 5% on your money-market account when you are being charged 19% on credit card debts!

Soon you will get used to this new attitude toward money management— and it is rewarding to see your savings grow.

Chapter 9
Dealing with consumer debts: Financial strategies

Cash flow management suggested guidelines:

When you follow these guidelines, you stay out of trouble and avoid straining yourself financially.

1. **You are learning to live on 90% of your take-home pay.** Every month, you are PAYING YOURSELF FIRST by taking 10% of your paycheck and depositing it into a savings or money market mutual fund. <u>As discussed, you should strive to accumulate about three months worth of living expenses reserves in case of a sudden lay-off, disability or sickness.</u>

2. **Your rent or mortgage payment should not exceed 30% of your gross pay.** This is a very common formula in the loan business and one that makes a lot of sense. So if you gross $2,000 month, you really ought to pay no more than $600 for rent.

3. **Your other installment and revolving debts (car payments, VISA, Discover, etc.) should not exceed 10 to 15% of your gross pay.** Once again, if your before-tax income is $2,000 a month, you can afford $300 a month to pay for your car PLUS all your other credit cards payments.

The reason most people get into financial trouble is because they constantly overextend themselves. Each month the credit card balances get bigger. Each month the savings account balance gets smaller. Soon things get out of hand!

Five simple ways to limit your credit card spending:

1. *Leave your credit cards at home if you are a compulsive shopper.* Oftentimes, the urge to buy that sweater or suit subsides after you get home and think about it twice.

2. *Get a VISA ATM debit card and use it in lieu of credit cards.* These new generation of bank ATM cards are being welcomed at most supermarkets and other retail stores.

3. *Make it a point to pay off all your cards within this year.* You won't be tempted to charge this way and you'll save a fortune on finance charges in the long run.

4. *Limit your credit cards to two or three at the most.* Pay the rest off as soon as can you can and close those accounts. You don't need to have a dozen cards charged to the hilt!

5. *Make it a policy to pay down your current balance on a card every month.* DO NOT GET INTO THE HABIT OF PAYING JUST THE MONTHLY MINIMUM DUE. Even if money is really tight for now, pay an extra $10 or $20 over the minimum due every month, otherwise you'll never crawl out of your credit card debt.

What if I am already neck deep in debt?

If you are a homeowner and have good credit: You may want to look into a home equity bill consolidation loan. You are in essence giving up your current and/or future home equity for the sake of getting some debt relief.

Let this be a lesson to you, and start re-evaluating your spending habits.

The best place to start looking for an equity line of credit or second mortgage is the bank you are currently doing business with. A new program offered by many mortgage loan brokerage companies offers a second mortgage up to 125% of your home's value minus your first mortgage balance. If you can pay off your existing balance gradually, you are wise to do it and leave your home's equity intact. However, if you are desperately in need of some debt relief this may be a viable alternative.

If you have a clean credit file: Try to refinance your *highest interest* credit cards. Although most banks offer you special "perks" for transferring you to their cards, most of these incentives are short-term and are nothing more than gimmicks to earn your business. Once again, you can contact Bankcard Holders of America for a list of low-rate credit cards. In most issues, *Money* magazine lists the top three or four banks with the lowest credit cards rates.

If you are married with only one spouse working: Does it make financial sense for the nonworking spouse to start working? If you have several children that need to be sent to day care to accomplish this, it may not be a practical solution; but you can weigh the options of having a full-time at-home parent, or one that works part-time and still meets the needs of the children.

If you are running out of options: Get a part-time job or start moonlighting on the side. If you can sew, fix computers, sell on the phone, do bookkeeping, paint houses, type, etc...<u>GET TO WORK</u>! Additionally, set up a budget to lessen your expenses as much as possible. Yes, I know it is hard, and what about weekends and quality time with your family? The good news is you'll learn your lesson and you will probably need to do this only for a few months or a year at the most. The more you procrastinate, the worse it gets. So take action now and make things easier on yourself.

Filing bankruptcy as a last resort

According to research done at Purdue University, the average person filing a Chapter 7 bankruptcy has a monthly after-tax income of $1,607 with monthly expenses of $1,711 and credit card debts in excess of $17,000. Am I starting off this section with this statement to encourage you to file bankruptcy if your situation resembles the above-mentioned profile? Quite the contrary.

My point is that we live in times where we are constantly being lured to apply for more and more credit. *Every person filing bankruptcy was once an individual with excellent credit.* Filing bankruptcy is a personal issue that requires careful consideration. Even though it may be the best or sometimes the only solution for extreme financial hardship, it should ONLY be considered as a LAST resort, since bankruptcy will have long-term financial consequences.

If you are considering filing a bankruptcy, you need to explore all your alternatives first to make sure that it is the proper thing for you to do. In the capacity of a mortgage consultant, I have come across many individuals who have filed bankruptcy for the most ridiculous reasons and have come to regret their decision later. The following section is designed to give you a basic understanding of the two types of bankruptcy plans available to individuals.

Chapter 13 bankruptcy: Also known as a debt-restructuring plan, this type of bankruptcy allows people with regular income who need to pay all or a major portion of their debts to be under the protection of the court. A Chapter 13 B/K allows you to keep all your assets while the plan is in effect, and after you have successfully completed it. It is available only to individuals who have less than $100,000 in unsecured debts, such as credit cards, and who have less than $350,000 in secured debts, such as car loans and mortgages.

The following are the major characteristics of a Chapter 13 B/K plan:

1. It is filed by approximately 20% of all those opting for a bankruptcy.
2. It can be used repeatedly.
3. It may allow payments in full for less than the amount originally owed.
4. Home and cars will be preserved if the plan is successfully completed. If not, they might be taken by creditors.
5. Repayment term is often three years to five years.
6. Borrower is no longer liable for most debts if plan successfully completed.
7. Record of bankruptcy will remain on credit record for up to ten years.

Chapter 7 bankruptcy plan: Such a plan allows you to discharge most debts without having to go through any repayment plans. Unlike a Chapter 13, there are no monetary limitations as far as the maximum amount of secured and unsecured debts are concerned Most personal bankruptcy cases fall within this category.

The major characteristics of a Chapter 7 B/K plan include:

1. It is filed by approximately 80% of those opting for a bankruptcy.

2. It can be used only once every six years.
3. Most debts are discharged with no further liabilities.
4. Whereas cars might be taken by creditors, your home may be preserved under homestead exemption and/or marital ownership law.
5. A record of the bankruptcy will remain on your credit record for up to ten years.

Your financial planning project for this coming weekend

Make it a point this coming weekend to set aside some time to sit down and devise a financial plan for yourself. The aim is to accomplish the following:

* **Start to SAVE at least 5% to 10% of your take-home pay.**

* **Use the suggestion's outlined in Chapter 8 to cut down your expenses and devise a realistic plan to pay off most of your credit card debts as soon as possible.**

* **Make a written commitment to yourself to pay off all your credit card debts by a realistic date. Then check your progress every month to see how much closer you are getting to your goal.**

After six months, celebrate (economically!) your achievement of greater financial solvency. You deserve to be proud of your consistent money-management skills and the accomplishment of a secure retirement.

Part V

Managing your biggest debt: Your mortgage

Chapter 10
Getting approved for a home loan

This section deals with the basics of getting you prepared for a home loan. At this stage, you should have resolved all or at least most of your credit issues, and re-evaluated your spending habits. A home loan is a tremendous responsibility. Blindly jumping into home ownership without carefully assessing your current financial situation can be devastating.

The home loan approval process

Home loan approval is somewhat different from obtaining most other lines of credit. For one thing, it involves a huge amount of paperwork. Just about every single piece of information on the handwritten application (Form 1003) is evidenced by supporting documents. The prospective borrower is asked to provide the lender with pay stubs, W-2 forms, bank statements, pink slips, as well as any bankruptcy papers, divorce decrees, gift letters, vehicle pink slips, and even tax returns, if applicable.

The loan package is first put together *(processed)*. Then it is sent to a loan underwriter who will spend an average of forty-five to sixty minutes reviewing the loan package to make sure it conforms with the lender's and/or the loan program's approved guidelines. He or she will hopefully issue a loan approval, which is often subject to several conditions. The loan officer and the loan processor(s) are then in charge of satisfying the conditions before loan documents can be ordered.

Because of its complexity, the home loan approval process is a relatively long and tedious process. It is thus important for a first-time home buyer to become familiar with what is needed over and above a clean credit profile.

The four big "C's" - requirements for a home loan

Capability: This refers to your income-producing capability and your current overall debt. How much you earn is evidenced by your pay stubs, W-2 forms and/or tax returns which in turn determine how big a loan you can afford.

Current revolving and installment debts are other limiting factors in qualifying for a bigger loan amount. The larger your current credit obligations, the less you can apportion toward housing payments. Lenders calculate your housing to income AND your total debt to income ratios to determine your eligibility for a requested loan amount.

Collateral: This refers to the property that will serve as the security for the loan. Most loan programs require the property to be in satisfactory condition, as evidenced by a home inspection and an appraisal report. Additionally, they require the prospective borrower to have at least a minimal amount of equity tied into the transaction. In other words, you must put down a down payment even if it is a fairly small one. The more money a borrower has tied up in a property, the less likely he or she is to walk away from it if things begin to get tough.

Character: Your credit, job and savings history are all indicative of your financial character. Prospective borrowers with "spotty" credit, unstable job histories and a lack of savings are not what lenders look for.

Cash on hand: This includes down payment money, funds to cover the home loan closing costs and any cash reserves left at the close of escrow. This area is often a source of problems and confusion for most home buyers. We will cover these in detail.

"To shine own self be true"

You owe it to yourself and your family to evaluate your current financial situation carefully to determine if you are truly ready to assume such a major, long-term liability. The subject of buying a house will often become a highly emotional issue for prospective buyers when common sense gets replaced by wants and desires. The following *"red flags"* should be taken very seriously.

DO NOT PROCEED:

If you are just starting on a new job or if there have been sudden layoffs within your department or company: Accepting a higher-paying position at another company with a better career outlook is one thing; changing jobs for any other reason is another. Don't make the mistake of burdening yourself with a home loan if you are not sure about your job future. Recent layoffs are also a bad sign. Proceed with extreme care and avoid losing your objectivity.

If you lack savings and/or are not even contributing to your employee-sponsored retirement plan at work: This can only mean that you are living from paycheck to paycheck! What happens if you become sick or disabled for a few months and cannot work? Spend a few months or even a year, if necessary, to beef up your savings. Besides, you do need to have a down payment and extra money for closing costs.

If there is trouble in paradise: This may sound far-fetched, but I cannot begin to tell you how many times I have witnessed it during my career as a loan consultant. Here it goes: Husband and wife have problems. They choose to believe it will go away. It doesn't. Next, a decision is made that a child is going to change things. No such luck. Finally, they figure a new home is what they really need. Sooner or later, everything comes crashing down like a wave and one spouse decides to leave while the other is stuck with mortgage payments that are now unaffordable. The rest is a sob story that I have heard way too many times over the years. Buying a house and getting a big home loan is not the remedy to a problem marriage.

If you have STILL have large credit card balances: Your debts will directly affect how much of a home loan you qualify for. I cannot begin to count the number of times I have sat down across the table from an applicant with $20,000 or $30,000 in accumulated credit card debt who wants to buy a house and hardly has any money for a down payment! Now, how much sense does that make?

Chapter 11
Home loan basics

The down payment

Today's home loan programs allow prospective home owners to get into a house with as little as 3% to 5% down. A few programs even allow 100% financing, but there are always stringent requirements to these no money down financing programs. Therefore, chances are that you do need to come up with a down payment.

Where you CANNOT get down payment money:

From an undocumented source: You can't tell a bank loan officer that you keep your down payment money in your bed pillow at home or in a safe deposit box! Down payment money must be "parked" in an account under your name for at least three months, or you must provide proof of how and where you got it. You simply cannot bring the "green" to the table at closing time!

By charging up your credit cards or by getting a personal bank loan: This would constitute a fully-leveraged transaction. The lender wants you to put some of your hard-earned money into the transaction so you won't walk away from the property at the first sign of trouble. Also, remember that your total debts directly affect your home loan affordability. Therefore, charging up your credit cards to come up with a down payment is not only futile but also unallowable under the home lending guidelines.

How to come up with down payment money

Get a gift from a parent or a close relative: A major portion of your down payment can come from gifted funds from mom or dad, your uncle Ben or Grandma Jenny. The standard in the lending business requires a minimum of 5% of your own funds, but there are plenty of exceptions to that rule. For example, FHA loans allow 100% of the down payment money to come from gifted funds. Also, if you are lucky enough to get a large gift that is equivalent to a 20% down payment, you do not have to come up with any funds of your own. The gift issue needs to be discussed with your loan officer early into the application process, since different loan programs have different guidelines regarding this issue. Note that gifted funds must have no obligation or repayment strings attached to them, otherwise they will be looked upon as loans.

Borrow against your cash value life insurance policies or the vested portion of your retirement plans at work: Old cash value life policies are an often-overlooked place to look for down payment funds. You can surrender your old policy or get a fairly low interest rate loan against it. The best part is that the loan does not need to be paid off. The amount of the loan outstanding will be deducted from the death benefit of the policy at the time of the insured's death. You may also be able to borrow from the vested portion of your 401(K) plan at work. Check with your human resources department about terms and feasibility. The PERS loans available to certain public employees allow the entire amount of the down payment to come from such a source.

Beware of this hidden tax trap: If you have money saved up in a tax-sheltered annuity, or most other retirement plans, think twice about dipping into these accounts by surrendering them. You will not only have to pay a 10% early withdrawal tax to the IRS, but you will also be taxed on any capital gains from such distributions. Before making such a move, discuss your intentions with your accountant or tax preparer.

Work out a rent-to-own lease with a seller: This is a fantastic option for someone who needs a "forced savings" approach to save up money for a down payment. Oftentimes, landlords are interested in this type of arrangement. Hint: If you are currently living in a rental house and would like to own it, you may want to discuss the possibility of a rent-to-own lease with your landlord.

Let's say that a seller (or your current landlord) is not in a big hurry to sell her house. If the comparable rent for a house of that size goes for $800 a month, you could talk the seller into a lease plan whereby you pay her $1,100 a month. She in turn agrees to credit the extra $300 toward your down payment. At the end of your lease in 12 or 18 months, you have accumulated anywhere between $4,800 to $7,200 toward a down payment.

In all likelihood the seller is going to insist that the lease contract specify that if you change your mind about buying the house during or after the term of the lease the accumulated down payment money will not be refundable to you. Despite this caveat, this is still a very good way to systematically save for a down payment.

Keep in mind that a home loan lender will insist upon seeing a written rent-to-own lease agreement and that the arrangement must be an arm's length transaction. For example: Let's assume comparable rents for a house in an area go for $600 a month. You cannot claim that $300 of that amount was earmarked toward down-payment credits. The lease agreement must make sense.

Save your IRS refunds and/or Christmas bonuses, and sign up for some overtime hours, if possible: These are excellent ways to save up for your dream home. Plan your work and work your plan. It may take you a few months or a year to get there, but the end result will be worth it!

Closing costs

In addition to your down payment, you will need additional funds to pay for your portion of the closing costs. Ordinarily, the seller of the property will pay for some, or in some cases, a major part of the related closing costs. These costs are dependent upon a variety of factors, such as your down payment, your loan amount, whether you elect to have impound accounts for your real estate taxes and insurance, and the origination/discount points of your home loan. *The law requires all lenders to provide you with a preliminary "good faith" estimate within three days of your application.* This estimate lists in advance all of the closing costs associated with a home loan. This is to help you be better prepared for all costs associated with a home loan. As its name implies, this form is simply an estimate, and NOT a guarantee of your final closing costs. You will receive a final and fully accurate "good faith" at the signing of your loan document.

Most common closing cost items

Origination fee: This fee covers the lender's administrative costs in processing the loan. Very often expressed as a percentage of the loan amount, the fee will vary according to lenders and/or interest rate market conditions. For example, one point on a $100,000 loan is 1% of this amount, or $1,000.

Loan discount fees: Also expressed a percentage of the loan amount, this fee is often used to buy down the interest rate on a loan. For example: You are quoted an 8.0% fixed rate by paying one point origination and zero discount points. The lender may also be able to offer you a lower interest rate, if you agree to pay discount points. In our example, you may choose a 7.75% fixed rate if you agree to pay one point for origination and one point for discount points.

Important note: Origination and discount points are sometimes bundled together. To find the best point /interest rate combination, you will need to take into consideration the additional costs involved versus the potential benefit (lower mortgage payments). Your loan professional should help you decide on this issue.

Credit report fee: This fee represents the cost of obtaining a residential mortgage credit report for your loan file.

Appraisal fee: This charge pays for an appraisal report for your loan file. Fees may vary from lender to lender. Also, the larger your loan amount, the more expensive the appraisal report is likely to be. While most reasonable lenders will provide you with a copy of this report, upon request, they are not required to do so unless state law covers this situation.

Inspection fee: This charge covers inspections required by the lender and/or the buyer. Next to an appraisal, obtaining a inspection report is a most vital step in determining that the property is free of any major defects such as lead-based paint, major termite damage, or other structural damage.

Mortgage insurance application fee: This type of insurance protects the lender against loss due to payment default by the borrower. It is applicable to a vast majority of loans that have less than a 20% down payment. The lender may require you to pay the first month's or the first year's premium in advance. FHA loans have both an up-front and a yearly mortgage insurance fee for single-family residence properties.

Assumption fees: This fee is charged in case the buyer is allowed and willing to take over the payments on the prior loan of the seller. Assumption privileges are most common on government and certain adjustable mortgages.

Processing/Underwriting fees or loan document fees: These fees compensate the lender and/or the loan broker for expenses associated with doing the necessary paperwork, reviewing and approving the loan package, and printing your loan documents.

Prepaid interest: Lenders require that borrowers pay at settlement the interest that accrues from that day, up to the beginning of the period covered by the first monthly payment. It usually takes at least thirty days for you to receive a coupon book; therefore the interest for that period is collected up-front at the close of your escrow.

Title insurance: The total cost of owner's and lender's can be bundled up or broken down. Title insurance protects both you and the lender against any and all losses due to problems or defects in connection with the title not identified by title search and examination.

Settlement or closing fee: This fee is paid to the settlement agent. Depending on the state you live in, this can be handled by an escrow company or an attorney. The closing agent is responsible for balancing out the transaction and dispersing the funds as well as coordinating the loan documents and funding procedures with the lender.

Impound account reserves: These accounts are required for most low down-payment loans. Impound accounts are set up for real estate taxes, fire insurance and/or mortgage insurance with adequate reserves to pay off these obligations as they come due.

The impound account reserve requirements often vary from one month to the next. If you have an impound account, you will contribute 1/12 of your real estate and insurance yearly dues each month, along with your principal and interest payment on your home loan.

Cash reserve requirements

Generally, home loan lenders do not like to see a borrower totally stripped of cash reserves at the close of escrow. Most loan program guidelines require a cash reserve of two to three months, equivalent to the mortgage payment. For example if your mortgage payments run about $800 a month, you ought to have at least $2,100 still left in the bank after your down payment and your share of closing costs. This requirement can sometimes be waived if there are compensating factors. Note that cash reserves are not a part of your closing costs.

Chapter 12
Deciding on a home loan program

Are you better off with a fixed rate or an adjustable?

A fixed rate is pretty straightforward. You maintain the same payment schedule, which makes the task of budgeting a lot easier. Furthermore, in an economic environment where interest rates are heading up, fixed rates offer you protection against rising interest rates. On the other hand, an adjustable allows you to start out with much lower payments. Oftentimes, it is somewhat easier to qualify for an adjustable if lenders use a lower qualifying interest rate than the going fixed rate.

Basically, with an adjustable loan, the borrower is assuming the interest rate risk for the sake of lower initial payments and/or easier qualification. Nowadays a vast percentage of individuals opt for an adjustable mortgage rate, especially with dozens of programs available to choose from. There are many different adjustable loan programs in the market, some of which have initial fixed rate periods as long as 10 years!

Other popular solutions include fixed rate balloon loan programs that offer 5 or 7 year fixed rates that are lower than 30 year fixed rates. These loans are very popular in California since the average Californian tends to move about once every five to seven years. These loan programs will always allow you to "extend" the term of the loan if certain conditions are met but very often at a higher rate.

Most prospective borrowers especially first time buyers tend to shy away from adjustable mortgages because they simply do not understand its mechanics. In picking a suitable adjustable rate, you cannot afford to be lurred by a low "teaser" rate. You must look at the overall picture very carefully.

The ABC's of an adjustable loan

Basically, an adjustable loan (ARM) has the following major characteristics:

Lower initial interest rates: ARMs offer lower initial interest rates than traditional fixed rate loans. Almost all adjustables start out with a "teaser rate" designed to attract borrowers. These initial rates will disappear within the first few months and the usual ARM rates will take effect. Therefore in shopping for an ARM look at the entire picture, not just the start rate!

Index & margin: Once the initial interest rate is established (after the teaser rate period,) the rate is tied to some "neutral" index. That means that the movement of the index is beyond the control of the borrower or the lender. Some popular indices include the 1 year treasury, the 6 months LIBOR, or the "cost of funds" of the 11th District of the Federal Home Loan Bank of San Francisco. The *margin* refers to the gap between the index and the interest charged to the borrower. The margin is always a constant, while rates change according to the fluctuations in the index.

Yearly and lifetime caps: Due to what is known as a "payment shock" most ARMs have interest rate caps, which are nothing more than a "ceiling" on annual and total interest increases. Most ARMs have a 2% yearly cap and a 5 or 6% total increase over the initial contract rate. For example, if an ARM starts out at 6.5% with a life cap of 6% the maximum interest it can go up to is 12.5%. A decent margin and a steady index is what is going to save you money in the long run.

Beware of negative amortization! It may make sense in some circumstances, but make sure you understand its potential consequences.

The negative amortization concept originated during times of high inflation which necessitated the need to qualify the borrowers at a low entry-level even though the payments would later increase to accommodate full amortization of the loan over its term.

In the case of negatively amortized loans, initial or even future payments are inadequate to satisfy the interest payment requirements. This means that not only your principal will not reduce with each payment; it will actually increase due to the fact that the interest rate shortfall will be added to it!

In simpler terms, you may end up owing more after a few years of making payments than when you started! Fortunately most of these loans will "recast" into a new amortized loan once a loan balance equates to 125% of the original debt.

Negative amortization may not be a bad short-term alternative for a borrower in a period of very high interest rates where properties are appreciating at a rate to 10 to 15% per year. The negative amortization damage will be minimized by the rapid amortization of the property.

My personal recommendation is to stay away from neg-am ARMs especially in slow real estate markets when some areas are actually experiencing property depreciation. Even if you are buying in the midst of a real estate boom, a negatively amortized loan should be considered only if you plan on selling your property within 5 years or less.

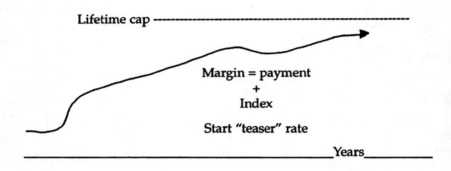

Graph illustrating an adjustable loan

Chapter 13
Popular government and conventional home loan programs requiring little or no down payment

Unlike obscure and complicated financing arrangements discussed in most zero-down manuals promoted by late night infomercial hosts, these programs should be easily available from most lenders in your area. They are easily implemented and offer very attractive rates and features.

The Veterans Administration loan programs

If you are a veteran with an honorable discharge, you are most likely eligible for this program. The VA loan is probably the most consumer-friendly loan program around. It requires only a $1.00 down payment. It also allows the seller or builder to pay for the closing costs so that you can move into a house with next to nothing. The VA Interest Reduction Rate Loan (IRRL) is the most fantastic loan refinance package around since it allows the veteran to refinance her mortgage with no appraisal required and no income qualification. As long as the borrower has paid her mortgage on time within the last 12 months and has no seconds on the house, she will be allowed to refinance her mortgage to a lower interest rate. This is often a godsend for a borrower who has experienced income or credit problems since closing escrow on the original loan.

The Housing and Urban Development loan program

Very popular programs among first-time buyers, FHA loans administered by the Department of Housing and Urban Development (HUD) allow a down payment of as little as 3% of the sales price. The entire sum needed to cover the down and the closing costs may be a gift from a relative. FHA guidelines are also more flexible on past credit problems and/or higher income to debt ratios. Like VA loans, FHAs also offer a refinance package with no appraisal and/or income qualification requirements if the purpose of the refinance is to lower your interest rate.

The Federal National Mortgage Corporation and the Federal Mortgage Home Loan Corporation (Fannie Mae & Freddie Mac)

Both of these conventional loan investors offer attractive loan down payment programs allowing prospective home owners to secure up to 95% financing on an owner-occupied property. Fannie Mae's *Community Home Buyer Programs* offer higher loan amounts than FHA loans ($227,150. vs. $160,950). Down payment is a minimum of 5% with 2% allowed in the form of a gift from a relative or a non-profit organization. This program comes in several different variations and has a strict income restriction depending on different geographical areas. Many lenders will also waive the reserve requirements on these programs if the borrower successfully completes an approved first-time buyer course prior to loan closing. These loan programs are often not limited to first-time buyers. Inquire about their availability and income restrictions in your area.

The Public Employee Retirement System loan program

This loan program is better known as the PERS loan. It is available to government employees who contribute to a

Public Employee Retirement System, and it allows 100% financing by letting the prospective home buyer borrow up to 5% of the sales price from the vested portion of her retirement account. The amount borrowed cannot exceed one-half of her vested funds in the account. If you are eligible for this loan, contact your human resources department for details about this program and a list of approved PERS lenders in your area.

The guaranteed rural housing home loans

This program is commonly known as the *"farm loan."* No, you do not have to be a farmer to qualify for this loan! This financing program is limited to rural areas having a population not in excess of 10,000, or not in excess of 20,000 if outside any Metropolitan Statistical Area (MSA). There are various lot size limitations that must be observed and you may have a hard time finding a lender that offers this program. However, it does allow 100% financing to qualified borrowers. This may be a viable option for you if you do not have any savings for a down payment and don't mind living in a rural area. This program also has an income limitation guideline similar to the Community Home buyer program discussed earlier.

Interest rate buy-down programs

From our previous discussion about interest rates and discount points, you should know by now that it is sometimes possible to buy down the interest rate on the loan (the note rate) by paying additional discount points. Buy-down programs take advantage of this very same principle. The discount points can be paid by the buyer, seller, builder or even the lender depending on the situation and/or program guidelines. The 2:1 buy down is the most popular version. Here is how it works: Let's suppose that the going rate for a fixed loan is about 8.5%. A 2:1 buy down allows a borrower to start out with an initial rate that is 2% below the market rate; in this case, a start rate of 6.5%. This rate subsequently will jump up to 7.5% in the second year and will "cap" out at 8.5% at the beginning of the third year. Its benefit to a borrower is twofold. First, it allows him to enjoy a lower rate for the first two years without having to opt for an adjustable rate loan. Second, it often allows the lender to qualify the borrower for a bigger loan by using the first year's rate in their ratio calculations (guidelines vary from one loan program to another). Make sure you understand how a proposed buy-down program works as well as how much its associated cost is, and who will pay for it before you agree to it.

80/10/10 financing programs

Strange name for a loan program if you haven't heard the term before— isn't it? 80/10/10's are simply a clever way to orchestrate a loan transaction and are perfectly acceptable to most lenders. An example will help explain the concept. Once again assume you have saved enough for a 5% down purchase transaction. Your parents also agree to give you another 5% as a gift. Now you have a 10% down payment, right? Next, the bank approves you for 80% financing on the property for sale. Wait a minute, you scream in a raging panic... You only have a 10% down payment, where are you going to get the other 10%?... Luckily, Nancy, the seller tells you not to worry. She will carry a second mortgage on the house equal to the additional 10% down needed.

Here is what the transaction will look like:
80% financing from the bank
10% second mortgage (seller carry) from Nancy

10% down payment (includes 5% of your hard-earned cash and the 5% gift from mom and dad) Now you see why it is called an 80/10/10?

Your next question probably is this: Why would the seller be willing to help me out? There may be several reasons. For one thing, the seller may not need all her money in a big lump sum. She may be more willing to lend you a part of it in return for monthly payments at a more attractive interest rate than bank certificate of deposits offer her. Nancy, our seller in the above example, would much rather carry a second on the house for a 10-year term with an interest of 11% than earn a meager 6% on the same money deposited in a bank CD. The seller could also be in desperate need to sell the house as quickly as possible, and if carrying a second could facilitate your loan approval process, she may indeed consider helping you out.

What happens if the seller is not willing to carry a second? Not to worry! There are plenty of lenders that will carry a second. A loan professional can easily help you find a suitable second mortgage program.

Finally, why on earth would you consider this kind of seemingly complicated arrangement? First, it is not complicated at all! 80/10/10's are easy to implement. Second, they do offer some very valuable benefits. For example:

Tax benefits: 80/10/10's do not require private mortgage insurance, better known as PMI. PMI is required coverage for the vast majority of home loans with less than a full 20% down payment. The purpose of it is to indemnify the lender for all, or at least a part, of the loan amount in case the borrower defaults on the loan and the property is forced into foreclosure. PMI insurance premiums, unlike the interest on a second mortgage are NOT tax deductible. Therefore, an 80/10/10 gives you a bigger tax deduction than a straight 90% loan with PMI coverage.

Program guideline restrictions: This usually happens with higher loan amounts (jumbo loans). The program's guideline may only allow up to 80% financing and you only have enough to make a 10% down payment. Obviously an 80/10/10 is the perfect solution to this dilemma.

Six easy ways to insure a smooth home loan transaction

Make sure you have cleaned up your credit profile as much as possible: Your files should be accurate, up to date, and as clean as you can get them prior to applying for the loan.

Avoid applying for any type of credit at least ninety days prior to applying for a home loan: You must remember our discussion about excessive inquiries signaling a red flag, and how they affect your FICO score.

Pay off as much of your credit card debts as possible a month or two prior to applying for the loan: You know by now that your revolving and installment debts will directly affect the size of the loan for which you could qualify. Additionally, some credit card companies take as long as 60 days to update your current balances on your credit files.

Avoid shifting money around: Since your down-payment money needs to be documented, you'll be doing yourself and your loan officer a great favor if you avoid shifting large sums of money around between your bank accounts. Postpone large cash expenditures until after the close of escrow.

Get pre-qualified for the loan prior to going out to look at properties: This will allow you to know accurately how much you can afford for a house. You may avoid the frustration of getting your offer approved by the seller, only to find out you can't qualify for that big a home loan. A proper pre-qualification means meeting with a loan officer and having her give you a prequalification letter. She will first have checked your credit, your income documents and your bank statements to make sure you have enough funds available for the down payment, closing costs and reserves. Do not settle for anything less than that. If the loan officer doesn't want to go through this process, then you need to find someone else to work with.

Do not apply for any more credit or change jobs after you have been pre-qualified: Opening up a large installment account is the surest way to mess up the loan process. Changing jobs may be acceptable if you are moving up to a better position and are staying in the same line of work, but it is to be avoided, if at all possible.

Prequalifying for a home loan made easy

This section is by no means intended to replace the process of getting pre-qualified by a loan professional. Its aim is to give you a fairly accurate idea of how big a home loan you can afford. It is primarily designed for salaried and hourly prospective borrowers. Also keep in mind that different loan programs have different ratio and credit guidelines.

Step 1: Income

Gross monthly salary or wages

Borrower 1 $ _____

Borrower 2   _____

Total: _____   (A)

                          (A) times .36 =   _____   (B)

Step 2: Debts

Auto payments

Car #1   _____

Car #2   _____

Credit card payments total
(Use minimum payments due):   _____

Student loans or other installment debts: _____

TOTAL MONTHLY DEBT PAYMENTS: _____   (C)

                     (C) minus (B): $ _____   (D)

(D) is the estimated maximum monthly mortgage payment you can qualify for!

Step 3:

Generally, 80% of your monthly mortgage payment covers your principal and interest. The other 20% covers real estate taxes and insurance, or any applicable homeowner's dues.

Therefore, to get your estimated principal and interest monthly payment, multiply (D) by .80.

(D) times .80 = $_____ (E)

(E) is the maximum principal and interest payment that you are likely to qualify for.

Step 4:

At this point you need to refer to the amortization table included in this section and figure out what loan amount (E) corresponds to the closest. For example, let's assume that (E) is equal to $800. Let's also assume that fixed rates are about 8.5% for a 30-year loan. After a few trial and error attempts it is easy to see that a loan amount of $105,000 (F) is a very close match.

Here is the math:
8.5% corresponds to a factor of 7.689 for a 30-year loan term
7.689 times 105 (loan amount) = $807.35, which is close enough!

As a loan officer, I rely on loan pre-qualification software. Doing it by hand will take a few attempts, but it is not a difficult task.

Step 5:

Lastly, to find out how much of a HOUSE you can afford, simply multiply the above number (F) by the proper factor.

For a 3% down payment, multiply (F) by 1.03 $ _____
For a 5% down payment, multiply (F) by 1.05   _____
For a 10% down payment, multiply (F) by 1.10   _____
For a 20% down payment, multiply (F) by 1.20   _____

IS THIS EASY, OR WHAT?

Equal Monthly Payment Per $1,000

TERM RATE	30 YRS.	15 YRS.	TERM RATE	30 YRS.	15 YRS.
3.000%	4.22	6.91	6.625%	6.40	8.75
3.125%	4.28	6.97	6.750%	6.49	8.85
3.250%	4.35	7.03	6.875%	6.57	8.92
3.375%	4.42	7.09	7.000%	6.66	8.99
3.500%	4.49	7.15	7.125%	6.74	9.06
3.625%	4.56	7.21	7.250%	6.82	9.13
3.750%	4.63	7.27	7.375%	6.91	9.20
3.875%	4.70	7.33	7.500%	6.99	9.27
4.000%	4.77	7.40	7.625%	7.08	9.34
4.125%	4.85	7.46	7.750%	7.16	9.41
4.250%	4.92	7.52	7.875%	7.25	9.48
4.375%	4.99	7.59	8.000%	7.34	9.56
4.500%	5.07	7.65	8.125%	7.42	9.63
4.625%	5.14	7.71	8.250%	7.51	9.70
4.750%	5.22	7.78	8.375%	7.60	9.77
4.875%	5.29	7.84	8.500%	7.69	9.85
5.000%	5.37	7.91	8.625%	7.78	9.92
5.125%	5.44	7.97	8.750%	7.87	9.99
5.250%	5.52	8.04	8.875%	7.96	10.07
5.375%	5.60	8.10	9.000%	8.05	10.14
5.500%	5.68	8.17	9.125%	8.14	10.22
5.625%	5.76	8.24	9.250%	8.23	10.29
5.750%	5.84	8.30	9.375%	8.32	10.37
5.875%	5.92	8.37	9.500%	8.41	10.44
6.000%	6.00	8.44	9.625%	8.50	10.52
6.125%	6.08	8.50	9.750%	8.59	10.59
6.250%	6.16	8.57	9.875%	8.68	10.67
6.375%	6.24	8.64	10.000%	8.76	10.75
6.500%	6.32	8.71			

Chapter 14
Mortgage loan reduction strategies: Part I.

The bi-weekly mortgage acceleration concept:

If you examine the truth-in-lending statement on any 30-year mortgage loan you'll soon discover that you will end up paying over 2 to 3 times your loan amount in interest expenses over the term of the loan. The exact numbers depend on your current interest rate and the term of the loan.

A simple and disciplined pre-payment strategy may not only reduce your loan term by a third or more, but will save you tens of thousands in unnecessary interest expenses. This in turn allows you to be mortgage-free by the time you retire, depending on your current age and the term of your loan. A mortgage acceleration payment plan is undoubtedly one of the most important financial planning tools you have available to you to ensure a comfortable and worry-free retirement.

How it works:

If you are about to buy a house: Find out if you can qualify for a 15 or 20-year term when you first take out the loan. Payments are usually about 25 to 30% higher than a 30-year loan, but you can save 50% or more on the interest payable over the long run.

If you currently have a 30-year mortgage: Call your lender and find out if they will accept your mortgage payments on a biweekly basis. You'll be making 26 payments, which translates into one additional payment over a year's time. This process will reduce the loan term by 9 to 12 years, and save you tens of thousands in interest. (See chart below.)

Example: A $150,000 mortgage at 8.5%, 30-year fixed.

	Regular mortgage	Bi-weekly mode
Paid off in:	30 years	22.5 years
Total interest:	$265,217.00	$187,607.00
Interest savings:	None	$77,610.00
No. of payments saved:	None	89 months
Gross payment savings:	None	$102,651.00
Average yearly interest savings:	None	$3,437.00

You may have no luck with your lender, or be told that the only way to go bi-weekly is to refinance your current mortgage. In this case, consider making an additional mortgage payment at the end of each year with specific instructions to the lender to apply the entire amount toward your principal. A less painful way is to find a reputable bi-weekly mortgage company acting as a third party administrator. Use caution in choosing the company. Check them out thoroughly before you sign up, since if they do not pay your mortgage payment on time, it will be reflected on your credit files and will negatively affect your credit rating

Another way to prepay your mortgage is to simply discipline yourself to send in an extra $100 to $200 over and above your regular mortgage payments. **You must include a separate note to instruct the lender to apply the additional payment toward** *principal reduction.* Any prepayment strategy is only effective if done on a consistent and long-term basis. Unfortunately, the vast majority of people adopting this powerful strategy will abandon it within a few months or a year; way too early to reap any real benefit from it.

A few wise clients of mine have even paid down their mortgage balances by a few thousand dollars when going through an interest-reduction refinance on their mortgage. This has always been endorsed by me. After all, why keep excess funds in a savings account and earn a meager 3% or 4% on them when you can pay down your mortgage and save thousands of dollars over the loan term?

An extra $50,000 or $100,000 saved in interest payments over a loan's term can mean that much more for you at retirement. Even if you don't plan to keep the house for the full 30-year term, you will still benefit from this strategy because you can build equity in your property up to 300% faster than the neighbor who pays his mortgage payments the regular way.

Chapter 15
Mortgage loan interest reduction strategies: Part II

Refinancing your mortgage

Refinancing to get a lower rate (rate & term):

The old rule of thumb says that there should be a reduction of at least 2% between the old and the new rate for the refinance to make sense. The truth is that even a .75% or 1% reduction in interest rate on a fairly large loan ($200,000 and up) may justify refinancing if other factors are present.

Factors to consider:

How long you are planning to keep the house?

If you are staying put for more than 4 years, it makes sense to refinance. If you are planning to put the house up for sale in a couple of years, the only reason you may want to refinance would be either because you simply cannot afford your current payments and need a break in interest to keep up, or that you have some sort of a balloon payment coming up and are not ready to sell the house yet. Other possible reasons are a need to get cash out of the property to pay off debts or for emergencies.

What are you refinancing into?

Are you refinancing into a better loan program or are you being lured into some "teaser rate" loan that will increase in the future causing you to pay as much (if not more) interest in the future? Compare the alternatives carefully. You want to better your financial position by taking on a new loan, not worsen it!

How many months will it take for you to "break even"?

Since the real costs of refinancing are the closing costs, you must determine how many months it will take you to make up for these expenses before realizing the "long-term" savings.

Use the following formula to find out your break-even point:

Old payment _____ <Minus> New lower payment _____ = Monthly savings

Closing costs even _____ <Divided by> Monthly savings _____ = No. of months to break

Refinancing to get "cash out":

You may need to refinance in order to pull some equity out of your property for a number of reasons, some of which might include:

Paying off high interest credit card debts.
Sending Jr. to college next semester.
Paying off the soon-to-be ex-spouse during divorce proceedings.
Starting out a new business or expanding an existing one, etc...

Most "cash out refinance" programs, as they are known in the business, allow you to borrow as much as 80% of the "appraised" value of your property.

In proceeding with a cash out refinance, keep the following points in mind:

If you have a low interest rate loan currently: It may make much better sense to take out a second deed of trust, also known as an "equity line of credit." Keep your first loan intact and get additional cash out through your line of equity, if feasible.

Evaluate the impact of the new loan carefully on your finances: If you are taking cash out to pay off credit card debts, you have to realize that you cannot do that every time you get yourself into trouble. If you are taking cash out to buy something, or to start a new business, how will the new payments affect your finances in the LONG RUN?

Don't buy a car or any other "depreciating asset" with a useful life of less than 15 or 20 years with the proceeds of a first deed of trust cash-out loan: If you are planning to buy a car, get a low rate line of equity that can be paid off in full after one or two years without incurring any prepayment penalties. Next, plan your payments in such a way as to pay off the entire balance in 4 years or less, just like a car loan. This way you may get a lower interest loan that may be tax deductible as well! (See your tax professional about the deductibility of interest.) It is not wise to refinance your entire outstanding loan balance over 30 years to take cash out for the purchase of a car that may only have a useful life of 6 to 8 years.

Determining the best rate/point combination in a refinance

Top choice: You have the cash and can pay for your closing costs and loan points with a check at escrow time.

Your loan balance is going to be less than if you roll over the closing costs into it. It also is a better arrangement from a tax planning point of view, because you may be able to deduct all of it at the end of the year. This is also an excellent time to pay down your principal balance by as much as you can afford. It will not only save you interest expenses over the long haul, but may also lower your new mortgage payments considerably.

Most common choice: Roll your closing costs and/or fees into the loan balance, provided you have enough equity in the property to do so. Oftentimes it is also better to pay about a point to buy the rate down, especially if you are planning to stay in that house for a long time.

As a last resort: Opt for a "no point and/or no fee" loan if you are short on equity or savings. Quite often, these loans have a significantly higher rate than the ones where you pay for closing costs and points. So don't be thrown off by the term "no point/no feel"! Remember, there is no magic to this. What the lender is offering you is to buy up the rate high enough so that enough rebate or servicing release premium can be generated to pay for all the fees. It is, however, a viable option, if you still are able to reduce your payments enough to make it worth your while to go through the hassle!

Second mortgages and lines of equity

Both the home equity line of credit and a second mortgage are similar in that the interest on both loans is tax deductible (up to $100,000 if you also meet some other criteria. Consult your tax professional.) Furthermore, your house will serve as collateral for both types of loans. Both loans will in essence be second liens against your property that must be paid off in full when you sell it.

The main difference between the two loans is that with a second mortgage, you usually get a lump sum for a fixed period of time, while a home equity loan is usually a "line of credit" with an adjustable rate on which you may draw over time.

If you need a lump sum of cash, or have less than perfect credit, you are probably better off with a second mortgage. If, on the other hand, you do not need all the money at once and do have good enough credit, an equity line of credit may be a better alternative since you won't be paying interest on the money until you actually withdraw it as needed.

It is a very sad fact that an increasing number of homeowners are in essence trading off hard earned equity buildup in their houses by taking up second mortgages. How much sense does it make to charge up last year's Hawaii vacation and all the crazy shopping sprees on the gold Visa only to have it paid off by taking up a second on the house?

Nevertheless, once the credit cards are charged up to the hilt, a second mortgage can often be a God send in order to allow homeowners to improve their monthly cash flow by consolidating all their credit cards debts into one, lower, tax deductible, second mortgage payment. A new generation of second mortgage programs now allow borrowers to get second mortgages up to 125% of the property's worth minus the loan outstanding on the first mortgage. Again, before you opt to apply for a bill consolidation second mortgage or equity line of credit, keep in mind that this loan needs to be paid off if/when you decide to sell the house!

Part VI

Car Financing

Chapter 16
Car leases and loan programs

Next to a mortgage, a car lease or loan is most people's second largest debt. When it comes to these financing plans, the caveat emptor (buyer beware) element is stronger than for almost any other consumer product there is, especially when it comes to a car lease.

Experts predict that by the turn of the century, over 40% of all new cars will be leased each year. Leasing already accounts for over 30% of all new cars sold in 1996, with more than half of these intended for personal rather than business use.

Is leasing a smarter alternative to traditional financing?

Leasing lets qualified customers pay for the portion of the vehicle that is used rather than pay for the entire vehicle, as you would with traditional financing. It can provide you with several attractive benefits, as follows.

Leasing provides lower up-front costs and lower monthly payments: Purchasing a vehicle often requires a fairly large down payment. According to Automotive News, new car prices have increased from an average of $12,526 in 1986 to over $17,000 in 1996. With car prices continuing to rise, a lease contract often allows your typical up-front costs to be as little as a refundable security deposit and your first month's payment. Furthermore, since you are paying for the portion of the value you use during your lease, rather than the entire value of the car, lease payments are usually lower than purchase agreements.

For example: Let's say you decide on a $20,000 car, and that the vehicle might be worth $9,000 at the end of the lease term. If you purchase the car using traditional financing, your payments will be based on the sale price of the new car, or $20,000. However if you lease the same vehicle, your monthly payments will be based on $11,000 which is the difference between the sales price and the estimated value at the end of the lease.

New car selling price	$20,000
Estimated value at end of lease term	$ 9,000
Lease payments are based on	$11,000

No resale hassles and a guaranteed purchase price: You will know up-front how much your car will be worth at the end of the term. You may buy the vehicle with a "deferred" payment at the end of the lease term if you decide to do so. Basically, if the market value of the vehicle is MORE than the guaranteed purchase price, you may want to buy the car. Otherwise, you can turn the car in with no further obligation.

Important tax advantages for the self-employed: If you are self-employed or a commission based salesperson, you may be able to deduct the full amount of each payment, including sales tax! You will have to amortize or deduct the amount of any down payment equally over the life of the lease. If you lease a "luxury" vehicle, one that costs more than $14,000, you will have to add to your income each year a certain amount for each year of the lease. The IRS has published a table that shows how much you would have to add to your gross income. Your accountant can most probably furnish you that information. However, the good news is that the increase in income is very small and its impact is often not noticeable due to the deductibility of the lease interest.

Buying or leasing... which is better for you?

Without a doubt a lease allows you to use more expensive cars for far less than what it costs you to "buy" them.

Take a look at this example and compare for yourself:

	Lease		Purchase
Selling price:	$16,995.00		$16,995.00
Down payment:	0		$ 1,700.00
Monthly payments:	$ 332.00		$ 486.00
Refundable security deposit:	$ 375.00		0
Amount due at delivery:	$ 707.00		$ 1,700.00
Number of payments:	36		36
Total payments	$11,952.00	vs	$19,196.00

Of course there are situations where your only choice is traditional financing. If your credit is not perfect or well-established, you may have a very difficult time getting approved for a lease. However you can still "buy" a car even if your credit profile is less than perfect.

If you opt to buy a car that is more than 3 or 4 years old, you will find traditional financing more economical in the long run.

Points to remember when getting a car loan:

If you do decide on traditional financing, keep the following points in mind.

Don't go over a 36-month term on your contract: First of all, you will pay more interest with a longer term. Second, if you total the car, you may get a settlement from your insurance company that will be based not on market value but on "actual cash value." For older cars, actual cash value is often far less than market value. That means you will realize a bigger loss than paid by your insurance proceeds. If you can't afford the payments based on a 36-month term, look at a less expensive car.

Get pre-approved for a car loan before you go out and buy the car: This is the same principle as with buying a home. Find out what you would like to buy, research its price, apply for the financing at your local bank or credit union; then go out and find the best deal on your intended vehicle. It is a lot easier and you are bound to get a much better deal this way. If your credit is spotty and you need a car in a hurry, you may want to look at dealers that offer special financing programs. You will end up paying a lot more not only on finance charges, but quite often for the vehicle itself.

Buy a car with an equity line of credit on your house: Although we have touched on this subject before, you need to be careful about several issues. First of all, I said an _equity line of credit, NOT a second mortgage._ It makes absolutely no sense whatsoever to buy a car that has an average useful life of six to eight years and pay for it over fifteen or even twenty years with a second mortgage. However, if you can secure an attractive rate on an equity line of credit on your house and plan your payments in such a way that you pay off the car in about three years or so, you may also enjoy the benefit of a tax deduction on the interest portion of the equity line of credit. Consult with your accountant before you proceed with this idea.

Are leases trickier than regular car loans?

Due to government's poor regulation of car leasing contracts, the language and terms used vary from dealer to dealer. Recent new federal regulations are beginning to make of shopping around for leasing plans a less onerous task for consumers. The Consumer Leasing Act requires agreements to include a statement of costs, covering areas such as amount and number of regular payments. It also now requires dealers to disclose terms such as insurance requirements. Early termination penalties are also to be spelled out in detail.

Five steps to obtaining a decent lease:

1. **Negotiate the car price first, making sure it is the same agreed upon amount specified in the lease:** If you ask a dealer how much the car's price will amount to, and you are told not to worry since it will come out to be the amount you want to allocate toward a monthly lease payment, it is time to consider getting up and taking your business elsewhere. This same principle holds true for a regular car loan. Know how much you are being charged for the car first!

2. **Know these key terms:**

    Capitalized cost: The car's sales price plus fees and taxes.

    The money factor: Used to calculate the interest portion of your monthly car lease payment.

    Residual value: The projected fair market value of the vehicle at the end of the lease term.

    Term: The length of time the lease will run.

    Closed end lease: At the end of the lease, you will not be responsible for any difference between the car's residual value and its fair market value.

Open end lease: Under this plan, you would be responsible for the difference if the vehicle's fair market value is less than the residual value.

Excess wear and tear: Damages or usage wear that you will be responsible for.

Gap insurance: Insurance coverage for the difference between the car's value and the lease balance if the vehicle gets damaged or stolen. This coverage is highly recommended since without it, you will be liable for the car under the early termination rules.

3. **Nail down the residual value:** This figure very typically ranges from 35% to 65% of the car's initial price. The more a car is worth at the end of the lease term, the lower your monthly payments will be. Therefore, it makes sense to choose a car with a high resale value.

4. *Ask about the money factor:* Leasing does cost money and you ought to know how much before you sign on the dotted line. Car leasing dealers use a money factor that may be converted to an approximate interest rate when multiplied by 2400. For instance, a money factor of 0.00354 converts to a rate of around 8.5%. The factor will vary from one leasing plan to another. It will also differ on one lease term to another.

5. *Check out the extra charges carefully:* A typical car lease allows 12,000 to 15,000 miles of driving every year. There is often a 10 to 25 cents per mile penalty for any amount over and above the allowed mileage limit. Are these limits compatible with your driving habits? Driving an extra 3,000 miles a year over the lease's allowed mileage limit can cost you an extra $1,800 at 20

cents a mile, over a three-year lease term. Another area to be careful about is a steep repair bill when your lease is up. Make absolutely sure that the manufacturer's warranty covers the entire term of the lease and the number of miles you are going to drive. Otherwise, you may be in for a nasty surprise.

The 1997 amendments to the federal Consumer Leasing Act:

The good news is that effective October 1997, dealers are required to provide you with all of the following information in writing.

1. The amount due at sign up including your capitalized cost reduction (down payment), the first monthly payment, any refundable security deposit as well as, all title, registration and other applicable fees (check these carefully!).

2. The date your monthly lease payments are due.

3. The step by step calculation used by the dealer to arrive at your monthly lease payments.

4. The total of all monthly lease payments.

5. All other applicable charges, such as disposition costs, if you do not buy the vehicle at the end of the lease.

Note: If you have opted for an open ended lease for the sake of smaller monthly payments, you really need to pay careful attention to item #5 above to avoid being on the hook for any unexpected balloon payments not correctly disclosed to you prior to making a buying decision.

Part VII

Bits and pieces

Chapter 17
Frequently asked questions

The significance of the APR:

Q) I keep seeing references to a term called APR. What does it signify?

A) APR stands for Annual Percentage Rate. Under the law, creditors must show you the amount being financed, the monthly payment, the number of monthly payments, and most important, the APR. You can think of the APR the same way you look at the price per pound in a fruit stand. For example: if the price of apples is fifty cents a pound, then you can buy a pound for one dollar, or four pounds for two dollars. In either case the price per pound is still fifty cents a pound.

Similarly, when you buy credit for a given number of months, the total dollar amount of your finance charges will depend on the size of your loan and its term. Keep in mind that an APR is NOT an interest rate. It is simply a uniformly accepted means of informing a borrower of the total cost of the loan. The problem that I see with the APR is that even most loan officers have a hard time understanding the concept. Also, despite the disclosure of an identical APR in two different credit card applications, each creditor may charge you very different finance charges every month. It depends on how you use the account and how they calculate the unpaid balance for assessing the charge.

When it comes to a home loan, I highly recommend that you request a good faith estimate from your lender and examine each cost item by item. Keep in mind that the APR is very often higher than the note rate on home loans, since it also factors in the costs associated with obtaining the credit (i.e., closing costs in a home loan).

Lost or stolen credit cards and credit card insurance plans:

Q) *I have always wondered about my liability in case I lose one of my credit cards. I often see little envelope stuffers with my credit card statements about credit card insurance plans covering my losses in case they get stolen. Should I enroll in such a plan just to be safe?*

A) I wouldn't spend money on the type of insurance plan you described. The Truth in Lending Act limits your liability on lost or stolen credit cards to the first $50 of unauthorized charges. There are also credit card plans that will cover your minimum monthly payments in case of a disability or involuntary lay off. If you pay your credit cards off as quickly as possible, like I suggested in this book, you should not have major problems making the payments during a distress period.

I believe everybody ought to invest in a quality long-term disability policy with an adequate benefit to cover not only credit card bills, but basic living expenses as well. The point here is to think more comprehensively about this issue and not to simply opt for a solution that takes care of a small part of the problem. You should also make copies of all your credit cards and keep them in a safe place, along with the creditors' toll-free numbers just in case you lose any of them.

Pre-approved credit card offers:

Q) *My mail box is filled with at least two or three offers a week for "pre-approved" credit cards that are unsolicited by me. What is going on, and is this to my benefit or not?*

A) Unfortunately, every time you receive an offer, an inquiry was made by the credit card company on your credit report. If you yourself are applying for credit to buy a car or a house, lenders will not be happy to see all of these inquiries, and may turn you down for the loan.

Until now there has been nothing you can do about it. Beginning September 30th, 1997, each of the credit bureaus will be required to let you refuse any of those pre-approved credit card offers. This is a provision of the new Fair Credit Reporting Act, and dedicated phone numbers for this purpose are: TransUnion, 800-680-7293; Experian, 800-353-0809; and Equifax, 800-755-3502. Call to request that your credit report be closed to pre-screening requests for two years. If you prefer, you can request that a form be mailed to you to close your credit report permanently.

Credit card convenience checks:

Q) I really like these new checks offered by one of my credit cards. Whenever I need some cash in a hurry, I can simply write a check and deposit it into my checking account. I did however notice that they only sent me a few, which makes me think that this must be a rather expensive way to get a cash advance. Is this a wise way to get cash for emergencies?

A) Use these checks only in case of an emergency where you cannot get money from any other source. By the time you add up all the interest and special processing fees, the cost of these checks can run as high as 30% to 40%! According to the Bankcard Holders of America, a $300 credit card check with a standard $2.50 fee and 18.5% interest will have an effective annual interest rate of about 33%!

To make matters worse, there is very often no grace period with these credit card checks. Interest starts to accrue as soon as the check is deposited into your account. That means that even if you pay off the entire amount by the next credit card statement, you will still be charged some interest. Additionally, there may be some other "junk fees" imposed on these checks. Use these checks with extreme caution, or better yet, destroy them as soon as you receive a batch so you won't be tempted! Beefing up your savings account is the better way to prepare for unexpected financial emergencies.

Resolving merchandise disputes:

Q) About two months ago, I ordered an electric tool by phone and charged it to my VISA card. When the merchandise arrived, I noticed right away that it was not what I had ordered. I sent it back as soon as I got the chance. I was still charged $195.00 for the returned item. I called the supplier and was told that they have no record of me sending the merchandise back. I finally told them to all go to hell and refused to pay for something I don't own. I am afraid this is going to damage my credit rating. How should I handle this?

A) This is a common dispute situation. The Fair Credit Billing Act requires creditors to correct errors promptly and without damage to your credit rating. A billing error includes a charge for:

1) Something you didn't buy in the first place but was charged to your account.
2) An item not properly identified on your bill or for an amount other than the actual purchase price.
3) An item that you did not accept on delivery or promptly returned because it was not delivered according to agreement.

Additionally, it covers situations such as failure of the creditor to mail a statement to your current address (provided you had notified them at least three weeks in advance). Some other questionable areas for which you need additional information fall into this category.

You need to address this situation promptly or it may very well damage your credit rating. You have taken the first step, which was to contact the creditor by phone. Obviously the dispute is still not resolved. Your next move is to send them a letter (see dispute letter #7). You MUST pay all parts of the bill that are NOT in dispute! If you have a large balance on the card and you are paying it off monthly, you must still make your minimum payment as it applies to all other charges on your card. The creditor must acknowledge your letter within 30 days. Within 90 days, either the account must be corrected, or they must provide you with a full explanation about the charge in question.

If the creditor made the mistake, you will owe no finance charges on the disputed amount and the account must be corrected. I would try to resolve the situation as quickly as possible in an amicable manner. Unfortunately the fact that they claim they never received the merchandise back from you is of no help here!

More about credit repair:

Q) You mentioned that it is prudent to dispute collection and charge-off accounts in batches. What about revolving and installment accounts that show late payments? Should I adopt the same approach?

A) Not really. Since you don't run any chance of the creditor restarting any collection efforts with late accounts, go ahead and dispute all of them at once. Of course if you have twenty late payment accounts you are trying to dispute, your request is going to look real suspicious, but there is no problem with disputing three or four in one dispute letter.

Q) I am just wondering whether previously deleted derogatory information can ever reappear on a credit report once it has been successfully disputed?

A) I have personally never run into this problem. Additionally, the new Federal Credit Repair Act does not allow a deleted item to be added again unless the creditor certified that the information is correct. If this ever happens in your case, and it is not a total impossibility, you would need to redispute the entry.

Q) I have been disputing this charge-off account for over six months now and the same thing happens every time -- I get an updated credit report and it is still there, yet I have not received any collection letters from them. I made an offer on a house last week What is the quickest way to get this thing off my credit report?

A) Pick up the phone and call any of the credit bureaus that are reporting this charge-off. Get the address and phone number of the creditor or collection company. Then use sample letter # 5 to negotiate a deal with them. This may take about three months from the time you write to them to the time they actually remove it from your credit reports.

As I am sure you know by now, you have to get them to commit in writing that they will remove the account from all the repositories once you pay them off. If you are in a hurry because you want to close escrow on a house, you can just pay it off in full, if it is a fairly small amount, but it will stay on your credit files.

A couple of small charge-off accounts are not detrimental to a home loan application if you have an otherwise clean and established credit profile. But if you already have a few dings on your credit, it may cause you to be declined for the loan. If you are not sure, ask your loan officer what to do about it.

Q) I have been trying to get this collection account off my credit files to no success. The creditor has sent me a few collection letters trying to get me to pay for this debt in full. I ignored the letters, and continued disputing the account. I was served yesterday with court papers. They are now suing me for the full amount plus court and attorney costs. I am scared. What should I do?

A) First of all, I have no problem saying that you and people like you deserve to get sued! The tools and techniques in this manual are for people who want to clean up their credit profile by paying off their debts. You seem to think that this manual is a passport for you to bully credit bureaus and creditors into deleting your derogatory credit information without you having to pay anything back. Well, you were obviously wrong.

As for your current situation, you still need to pay off your debt. I suggest you hire an attorney and settle out of court. The only difference now is that not only do you have to pay for an attorney, you will likely have to pay the full amount. Additionally, you can forget about being able to remove the entry from your reports for good. Be smart next time and settle the debt like I suggest.

Q) *I have a car repossession on my credit files that is four years old. It shows an amount outstanding of $7,000. Additionally, I have a few more charge-offs and am planning to get them removed according to your suggestions in this manual. My concern is this: The creditor has never tried to collect anything from me in relation to this account. If I dispute this account, I am afraid I'll be opening a can of worms. What do you suggest?*

A) The fact that the creditor never contacted you after the repo and the fact that it is over four years old are two things to your advantage. My suggestion is this: first focus on all your other charge-offs and get your credit files cleaned up except for the repo account. After you have done what you planned to do with everything else, then and only then, make a decision whether you want to take an aggressive or a conservative approach toward the repo account. The aggressive way is to dispute it and try to get it off. It may or may not happen. Because this is a rather large open charge-off, you may end up hiring an attorney to settle the matter the same way as any other charge-off account. If you want to adopt a conservative approach, then add a consumer statement next to the account and explain why it happened.

Good credit & employment:

Q) I was turned down for a higher-paying job at another company last week because of some credit problems I am still trying to sort out. I am a perfect match for the job as far as work experience is concerned, and find it really unfair that I was passed over simply because of some past credit problems. Can they really deny me employment because of my credit?

A) Yes... As of Sept. 1997, a new federal law requires employers to tell applicants if a credit report will be used as part of the hiring process. Additionally, they must disclose to applicants their rights, which include the ability to dispute inaccurate information on any credit reports. If turned down for a position, the candidate has the right to reapply for that position.

I personally never understood what a spotty credit report has to do with an individual's ability to perform a task. As far as I am concerned, unless someone is going to extend you credit, they have no business looking at your credit report!

I remember when lie detector tests were getting fashionable in the early 1980's as an employment screening tool, but now they are almost extinct, except if you want to apply for a job as a government agent or perhaps a police officer. I suspect that this practice of running credit reports on job applicants will sooner or later become a thing of the past after a few major court cases!

This employment-credit report problem is also a Catch-22 situation. How is one going to settle back debts if every time you apply for a higher-paying job, you get turned down because of bad credit?

Relatives or husband and wife credit issues:

Q) I have lived with my older sister for about a year since my divorce. Lately, I have been turned down for a car loan and a credit card due to derogatory credit. I have always strived to pay all my bills on time even in the midst of my divorce. I called and got my credit report, only to find out that all the collection accounts are my sister's! Will this ever occur again if I write to that bureau and explain the situation?

A) Make sure you include your current address for them to update their records. Once the situation is resolved, you shouldn't have any further problems with this issue. I suggest you obtain a new copy of your reports every year to make sure everything is kept up to date and accurate on your credit files. Also make sure you contact all other credit bureaus as well.

Q) My good-for-nothing ex-husband has incurred a bunch of unpaid tax liens that are now being reflected on my credit files as well. These tax liens happened after our divorce. Can I dispute these tax liens and get them off my credit reports?

A) Absolutely. Use the same procedure you would to remove any other inaccurate info from your reports. If they don't come off the first time around, send a second letter immediately and enclose a copy of your final divorce decree as proof.

Q) My soon to be ex-wife went berserk prior to our separation and ran up over $5,000 on one of our joint credit card accounts. Am I still responsible for paying these bills?

A) You should address this issue with your attorney and in your final divorce decree. If you end up assuming this debt, then you should contact the credit card company as soon as possible in writing and notify them that she no longer is an authorized user on that account.

Q) My husband left me and my child a few months ago and moved to another state. I am now receiving calls from bill collectors for items he charged on our joint accounts a few months ago. He still has possession of the cards. Am I responsible for these charges?

A) Yes! -- since your name is on the accounts as well. Your salvation is to file a divorce and address this issue as part of your divorce settlement. Meanwhile it is quite possible that this incident will affect your credit rating. Once resolved, you may want to add a consumer statement on your credit files explaining the circumstances regarding the lates.

Q) Will the fact that my ex-wife just filed a Chapter 7 bankruptcy affect my credit rating? We have been divorced for over a year now.

A) You're safe. The Equal Credit Opportunity Act requires creditors to consider applicants based on their own creditworthiness, not their spouse's or ex-spouse's. Just to be on the safe side, order your credit reports in a couple of months, and check them for any inaccurate information.

Q) If I get divorced can my home loan lender make me reapply for an existing loan because of my marital status?

A) Of course not.

Q) I am planning to marry my fiancé next month Unfortunately he has bad credit. Should we keep our credit matters separate while he works on his credit profile?

A) Oh, yes! Do not apply for joint credit, and continue to use your own last name. If he cleans up his credit completely, then you may want to consider applying for some joint credit.

Home loan credit issues:

Q) We were planning to make an offer on a property last week. Now we are being told by our bank's loan officer that we don't qualify for a home loan because of our credit. What recourse do we have to remedy this situation?

A) You put the carriage before the horse. The correct procedure is to get pre-qualified for a home loan to find out how much of a house you can afford based on your income, and to address any credit issues. There are a number of non-conforming loan programs that allow borrowers to get a home loan based on a 20 to 35% down payment, depending on your credit, but they are rather expensive. If you don't have that kind of cash for a down payment, work on your credit issues first, then get pre-qualified for a home loan before you go out and make any offers.

Q) I am in the process of getting a home loan and the lender is telling me that I need to pay off a $2,000 charge-off. I had a big fight with that creditor several years ago and I refuse to pay these jerks a red cent. What is your solution for me?

A) Pay off your collection account, or forget about being a homeowner. NO lender will extend you a home loan with an open charge-off.

Q) My credit is spotty and I have also filed a bankruptcy a few years ago. I am using a loan broker to secure financing on a property I intend to buy. Since I currently make good money and have no problem putting 25% down my broker is telling me about a lender that offers an adjustable loan that is about two percent higher than the market rate but does not care about my credit derogs and bankruptcy. Is this a worthwhile route to pursue?

A) There are an increasing number of "non-conventional" lenders that specialize in giving loans to credit-challenged prospective borrowers. I feel that they do provide a needed service that was only available a few years ago at an exorbitant cost. However, many people, especially first-time buyers do not have enough savings to afford a 20% or 25% down payment. People in this category should concentrate on repairing their credit as much as possible prior to applying for a low down payment mortgage.

I do caution you however, to stay away from non-conventional adjustable loans because most can easily shoot up to 16% or even 18% within a few years if rates start to go up rapidly. Many non-conventional lenders do also offer fixed rates.

I myself have mixed feelings about these loan programs. One must question the common sense of a prospective borrower with <u>continuing</u> credit problems to apply for a home loan in the first place. Many advocates of these programs argue that most of these programs are basically "band aid" loans that allow consumers to get needed financing while they work on improving their credit profile. As good as this may sound, I am not aware of many cases in which this argument has held true in practice.

Q) I have always saved and paid cash for everything, including two used cars I bought over the past ten years. I am now seriously thinking about buying a condo, and now I need a home loan. Can I be approved for a mortgage for $77,000 even though I have no credit history?

A) As I mentioned before, no credit is usually considered good credit. Since you are not asking for a very large home loan, you may well qualify for one if you have sufficient income and enough savings to cover your down payment and the closing costs. You will need to submit about twelve months worth of utilities, cable T.V. and car insurance bills. These will show your loan officer that you pay your obligations on time. He or she can then include these bills in your loan package as an "alternate" credit profile for you.

How to handle rude bill collectors:

Q) This bill collector is calling me relentlessly to collect a fairly recent large medical bill. He has called my wife and introduced himself as a "litigator" and has talked down to her without using any profanities. He has threatened me with wage garnishments and has made a derogatory remark about my country of origin. I hate this guy and cannot put up with his abuse. How can I stop him from calling me?

A) The Fair Debt Collection Practices Act was passed by Congress in order to protect consumers against the abusive and unethical practices of bill collectors. The following are examples of what bill collectors CANNOT do:
1. Use a false name.
2. Pretend to be an attorney, government official or credit bureau employee.
3. Claim your wages or property will be seized unless they really have the capability and intent to do so.
4. Claim that you will get arrested because you committed a crime. (That is, unless you have bounced a whole bunch of checks.)

5. Harass you at work or at home, especially after hours.
6. Call your boss and tell him you are a deadbeat.
7. Send you postcards or letters in envelopes that clearly indicate the sender is in the collection business.

It seems that this guy has crossed a few lines here. First send him a certified, return-receipt letter telling him to stop contacting you by phone or you will file a complaint with your state attorney general's office (see sample letter #8). He had no right to talk to you or your wife in the manner you described. You may then want to look into contacting the creditor and negotiating an affordable payment schedule.

Fair Isaacs credit risk scores revisited:

Q) Will my credit risk scores change once I clean up my credit files?

A) Of course! It will likely take ninety days or more. Your credit scores do change from time-to-time, based on factors already discussed, for the better or for the worse.

Q) You mentioned that many loan officers and lenders will not disclose my credit scores. Why is that? How can I improve my score if I can't know what it is currently?

A) Credit scoring is only one of the many things lenders look at. As we see in the section on home loans, income, debt-to-income ratios, your collateral (the house) and your loan-to-value position are other variables to be considered. As mentioned, the Fair Isaacs risk model was devised as an internal tool to help lenders with their decision-making process. That is why it is often not disclosed to the consumer. Additionally, you don't need to know your score to improve it. I already covered the factors that affect your risk scores. Pay your bills on time. Pay down your credit card balances as quickly as possible, and don't go chasing for additional lines of credit all over town, and your credit scores will be just fine!

Q) Do all lenders use these risk scores in approving credit?

A) Not every lender uses them as part of the approval process but a large majority do. Also, at the time of this writing, these risk scores are not used for government home loans such as VA or FHA.

Bankruptcy issues:

Q) I owe over $10,000 in back due credit card bills and taxes. Additionally, a business creditor just obtained a $7,000 judgement against me last month. Since I am a sole proprietor, I am fully responsible for this amount. I am seriously considering filing bankruptcy. Please tell me if this is a good decision, and if so, can I save money by filing bankruptcy myself?

A) I do not practice law! I will not give you any advice regarding whether or not to file bankruptcy. I will suggest that you review the bankruptcy outline section in this book and contact an attorney who specializes in bankruptcy cases to discuss your situation in detail. Keep in mind that regardless of what he or she may tell you, filing B/K is a very personal decision. If you get the slightest feeling that you are not getting fair and unbiased legal advice, get a second opinion. Also, it is wise to explore other alternatives to filing a B/K. Filing a Chapter 7 is not the solution to every financial crisis.

Q) How does a home loan lender view a Chapter 7 bankruptcy?

A) It must be discharged for at least two years and the prospective borrower must have reestablished at least two or more lines of credit without ANY lates. No derogs are allowed past the bankruptcy date. As mentioned before, some non-conforming lenders have less stringent guidelines but do require a bigger down payment along with a higher rate and points charged. Discuss your situation with a competent loan officer.

Where to turn for more help:

Q) I am getting more buried in debt each month, because of the inability to stick to a budget. I really need some outside help to set me straight before I am forced to file bankruptcy. Where can I turn?

A) If you need help with budgeting and cash flow management, try the *Consumer Credit Counseling Bureau*, a non-profit organization with offices nationwide at (800) 388-2227. Additionally, *Debtors Anonymous* is a free support group for anyone with debt or spending problems. You can obtain a meeting list by writing to: Debtors Anonymous, P.O. Box 20322, NY, NY 10025-9992.

Chapter 18
How to file a complaint

The Federal Trade Commission

Complaints about consumer credit reporting agencies, debt collection agencies, as well as violations of the Truth in Lending Act should be filed with the Federal Trade Commission. Keep in mind that retail companies, department stores, small loan and finance companies, state credit unions, public utility companies, and travel and entertainment companies are all subject to the requirements of the Truth in Lending Act.

Mail complaints to: Federal Trade Commission
Correspondence Branch
6th Street & Pennsylvania Ave, N.W.
Washington, D.C. 20530

Alternatively, you can send the complaint to one of the regional offices listed below:

Suite 1000
1718 Peachtree Street, N.W.
Atlanta, GA 30367
(404) 347-4836

Suite 810
101 Merrimac Street
Boston, MA 02114
(617) 424-5960

Suite 1860
55 East Monroe Street
Chicago, IL 60603
(312) 353-8156

Suite 520-A
668 Euclid Ave.
Cleveland, OH 44114

Suite 500
100 North Central Expressway
Dallas, TX 75201
(214) 767-5501

Suite 2900
1405 Curtis Street
Denver, CO 80202
(303) 844-2271

Suite 13209
11000 Wilshire Blvd.
Los Angeles, CA 90024
(310) 575-7575

Suite 1300
150 William Street
NY, NY 10038
(212) 264-1207

Suite 570
901 Market Street
San Francisco, CA 94103
(415) 744-7920

2806 Federal Building
915 Second Ave.
Seattle, WA 98174
(206) 220-6363

Comptroller of the Currency

All complaints regarding banks where the word "*National*" or the initials *N.A.* or *N.S.T.A.* appear in the institution's name should be forwarded to:
> Comptroller of the Currency
> Consumer Affairs
> 250 E. Street, S.W.
> Washington D.C. 20219
> (202) 622-2000

The Federal Reserve Board

This regulatory entity can handle state-chartered bank complaints. The banking institution must be FDIC-insured.
Write to:
> Federal Reserve Board
> Division of Consumer Affairs
> 20th and Constitution Ave., N.W.
> Washington, D.C. 20551
> (202) 452-3000

You can also contact one of the following regional branches:

104 Marietta Street, N.W.
Atlanta, GA 30303
(404) 521-8500

600 Atlantic Ave.
Boston, MA 02106
(617) 973-3000

P.O. Box 0387
Cleveland, OH 44101
(216) 579-2000

2200 North Pearl
Dallas, TX 75201
(214) 922-6000

925 Grand Blvd.
Kansas City, MO 64198
(816) 881-2000

250 Marquette Ave.
Minneapolis, MN 55401
(612) 340-2345

33 Liberty Street
NY, NY 10045
(212) 574-6116

10 Independence Mall
Philadelphia, PA 19105
(215) 574-6116

P.O. Box 27622
Richmond, VA 23261
(804) 697-8000

P.O Box 7702
San Francisco, CA 94120
(415) 974-2000

P.O Box 442
St. Louis, MO 63166
(314) 444-8444

Additionally, the FDIC operates a toll-free telephone hotline for consumers in need of guidance. This allows the public to ask questions or offer complaints about consumer-related matters involving all FDIC-supervised banks. The toll-free number is (800) 424-5488. Its daily servicing hours are Monday through Friday from 9:00 AM to 4:00 PM, Eastern Time.

The National Credit Union Administration

This government entity handles most complaints about federal credit unions. Write to:
>National Credit Union Administration
>1775 Duke Street
>Alexandria, VA 22314
>(703) 518-6300

Part VIII

Sample dispute letters

Sample letter #1:
Requesting a copy of your credit report from a credit repository

Equifax
P.O. Box 740241
Atlanta, GA 30374

[Today's date]

Dear Sirs:

I am requesting a copy of my credit report to make sure that the information you have in my file is accurate and up to date. I further understand that I can order my credit report at no charge once a year.

[Signature here]

John Chang
Soc. Sec. #: 215-98-6565
D.O.B: 01/06/59
Address: 712 Brooklyn St., Apt. 12
Anytown, CA 49678

Sample letter #2:
General dispute letter

Transunion
P.O. Box 390
Springfield, PA 19064

[Today's date]

Dear Sir/Madam:

I am writing to you regarding several items on my credit report that need to be addressed immediately:
1) My social security number is 215-98-6565, NOT 215-98-6555. Please refer to a copy of my social security number card and driver's license number for proof.

Additionally, I request that the following items be investigated immediately as they are highly injurious to my credit rating. These creditors must provide you with WRITTEN & VERIFIABLE proof that these accounts belong to me, otherwise they must be removed from my credit file.
2) ABC collection, account #33456-890-0 for $750.00
3) E-Z Credit Inc., collection account #3678999 for $45.00
4) Sleazy Inc. Collection Services, account # 000987 for $310.00

I greatly appreciate your prompt attention to this matter and look forward to receiving an updated copy of my TU credit report within the next 30 days.

Sincerely,
[Signature here]

Julie L. Smith
Soc. Sec. No.: 215-98-6005
D.O.B: 01/06/59
Address: 712 Brooklyn St., Apt. 12
Anytown, CA 49678

Sample letter #3:
Follow-up to letter #2

Equifax
P.O. Box 740241
Atlanta, GA 30374

[Today's date]

Dear Sir/Madam:

On 07/09/96 I sent you a letter disputing several collection accounts on my credit report (see copy enclosed). This letter was received by your company on 07/14/97 (see copy of certified, return receipt, enclosed).

According to the Fair Credit Reporting Act, you have 30 days to investigate any disputed items on my credit file. If you are unable to verify that the disputed items are accurate and belong to me, you are required by law to remove them from my credit report.

It has now been well over 30 days since Equifax received my dispute letter and I have not yet heard back from you. I demand an immediate answer to my dispute letter. Either provide me with written, verifiable proof that the disputed items are accurate and do belong to me, or remove them from my credit report as they have damaged my credit rating.

Thank you for your prompt attention to this matter.

[Signature here]

John X. Shafdt
Soc. Sec. No.: 210-12-6265
D.O.B: 01/09/67
123-A 1st St., S.W.
Oakland, CA 90788

Sample letter #4:
Second effort letter

Equifax
P.O. Box 740241
Atlanta, GA 30374

[Today's date]

Sir/Madam:

I just received a new copy of my credit report and correspondence indicating that you have investigated the following disputed items on my credit file with TRW:

1) XYZ collection account #456009 for $350.00
2) Cars-R-Us account #345-00-9A, rated as a repossession
3) VISA account number 45687899999 rated as two times 30-days late and two times 60-days late.

I am entitled to know where and from whom you are getting this information, since your company is reporting information that is unverified to potential creditors! I have specifically asked you to obtain **written and verifiable** proof from these creditors that these accounts belong to me and are being reported correctly. Obviously you have not done so. I therefore request that you furnish me with the following:

1. The phone numbers and complete addresses of these creditors, as well as the full name and position of the individual in each organization that you have contacted to verify this debt.
2. Copies of any proof showing that these accounts belong to me, such as a contract or signed charge slips.
3. Proof that these accounts have been rated accurately, such as a complete payment history on these accounts.

If the creditors are unwilling or unable to cooperate, then you need to remove these derogatory entries from my credit profile. The rating on this account has affected my creditworthiness. This situation needs to be resolved as soon as possible. I am making reasonable demands in regard to these accounts. I do have a right as a consumer to verify that the information you are presenting to my creditors is correct and verified.

[Signature here]

Shariffah Goldberg
Soc. Sec. No.: 345-00-9876
D.O.B: 9/9/61
Address: 56 E. 158th St.,
NY, NY 09812

Sample letter #5:
To be used to negotiate an existing collection or charge-off account

Credit Max Inc.
P.O. Box 777
Susanville, CA 89096

[Today's date]

Dear Sirs:

    I am writing you in reference to collection account #445677890 for $978.00, currently on my TRW and Transunion credit files. I would like to pay off this account in **FULL** by making three (3) equal and consecutive monthly payments of $190.00. Since this collection account is over four years old, I believe this is a win-win situation for both parties. I do however have one condition for this settlement: **You must state to me in WRITING within the next fifteen days that you agree to remove this collection account from all the credit bureaus you reported it to, no later than a month after my last payment.**
    I will make the first payment upon receipt of this written agreement, and every month thereafter until this account is settled in full as described above. Please reply to me promptly.

Sincerely,
[Signature here]

Patrick B. Ratt
567 Helms Ct.
Paris, TX 07823

Sample letter #6:
Used to add a consumer statement to a credit file

TRW
P.O. Box 2106
Allen, TX 75002

[Today's date]

Dear Sirs:

I would like to add the following consumer statement to my credit report.
"On December of 1993, I severely injured my back in a work-related accident and had to live on my workman's compensation income for over four months. In addition, I could no longer perform the duties of my old position and had to eventually get another job in a different line of work. I tried my hardest to keep up with all my financial obligations during this crisis period. I contacted Repos-R-Us, my car lender, to work out an alternate payment plan for the short run, but they were very rude and uncooperative. As a result, I fell behind in my car payments and the vehicle was repossessed a short time later. They did not make the slightest effort to help me keep up with my payments. This explanation is most important in countering the unjust and rude manner I was treated by this creditor. Thanks to a lot of hard work and a tight budget, I have since increased my savings and will not be caught off guard ever again."
Please send me an updated copy of my report including the above statement.

Sincerely,

Xavier M. McCloud
Soc. Sec. No.: 009-00-9876
D.O.B.: 9/13/56
567 Treat Way, Apt. 4A
Cincinnati, OH 98654

Sample letter #7:
Used to dispute an item or entry directly with a creditor

Triple A Jewelers, Inc.
1000 Main Rd.
Floyd, MA 05667

[Today's date]

Regarding account #012235556

Dear Sirs:

My account statement dated 5/1/94 contains a charge in the amount of $265.00 for a diamond ring which was returned to your Central Avenue store, where it was originally bought on 3/20/94. I have stopped by that store, and the store assistant manager Robert has assured me that this item will be corrected on my next statement.

Please investigate this matter immediately and make the necessary correction as soon as possible. This account is under my own name and should have a zero balance. If you need to talk to me regarding this matter, you may call me at 213-555-0989.

Sincerely,
[Signature here]

John Edward Mead
234 45th Ave., N.W.
Washington, D.C. 06234

Sample letter #8:
Used to stop a nasty bill collector from harassing you

Mr. Eddie Carmichael
Sleaz Bag Collection Co.
122 Boyd Rd., No. 100
Oakland, CA 94598

[Today's date]

Mr. Carmichael:

Following our telephone conversation today, I hereby request that you end all telephone communications with me at home or work. Your manners are rude and in violation of the Fair Collection Practices Act. Further harassment from you will result in my filing a complaint with the Attorney General's office.

Sincerely,
[Signature here]

Shaun Shadmond
766 Concord Av., Apt. 3
Concord, CA 94596

Index

Adjustable loan	74
Appraisal fee	69
APR	109
ARM (See adjustable)	
Assumption fee	70
Bankcard Holders of America	21
Bankruptcy	20, 56, 123
Beacon	9
Bi-weekly Mortgage	87
Bill collectors	121
Break even	92
Capability	62
Capitalized cost	103
Caps	74
Car leases	109
Cash out refinance	92
Cash reserves	41
Chapter 13 B/K	56
Chapter 7 B/K	57, 123
Character	62
Citibank	44
Closed and lease	103
Closing costs	68
Comptroller of currency	127
Consumer credit counseling	25, 124
Consumer Leasing Act	105
Consumer statements	41
Convenience checks	111
Credit bureaus	3, 6, 10
Credit cards	13, 21, 110, 111
Credit history	5
Credit repair	25, 31, 39, 113
Credit repair organization act	27
Cross Country bank	20
Debtors Anonymous	124
Deferment	43
Dispute letters	132, 133, 134, 135, 136, 137, 138, 139, 140
Down payment	66, 120
Eighty/Ten/Ten financing	80

Equifax	7, 9, 111
Equity lines of credit	95, 102
Establishing credit	19
Excess wear & tear	104
Experian (see TRW)	
Fair credit billing act	4
Fair credit reporting act	4
Fair debt collection act	4, 121
Fair Isaac's scoring model	9, 122
Federal Consumer Leasing Act	4, 105
Federal Direct Consolidation Information Center	44
Federal Mortgage Home Loan Corp.	78
Federal National Mortgage Corp.	11, 78
Federal Reserve Board	127
FHA	78
FICO (see Fair Isaac's)	
Fixed rates	73
Gap insurance	104
Government Student Loans	42
Graduated payments	43
Help	124
Home loans	61, 73, 77, 84, 89, 119
Housing & Urban Development loan (see FHA)	
Husband & wife issues	117
Impound reserves	71
Income based repayment	43
Index	74
Inquiries	5
Inspection fee	69
Installment debts	39, 53
Insurance (credit cards)	110
Interest rate buy downs	79
Margin	74
Merchandise disputes	112
Mortgage acceleration	88
Mortgage insurance (M.I.)	81
National Credit Union Administration	129
Negative amortization	75
Open end lease	104, 105
Pay yourself	51
Point scoring system	13
Pre-approved card offers	110

Pre-qualification	82, 84
Prepaid interest	70
Processing fee	70
Public Employee Retirement System (PERS)	78
Public records	5, 39
Rate & Term refinance	91
Rate/point combinations	93
Re-establishing credit	19
Refinancing	55, 91
Rehabilitation	44
Reinstatement	44
Repositories	3, 31
Residual value	103
Revolving debts	39
Sallie Mae	44
Second mortgages	94
Secretary of Education	44
Secured credit cards	19, 21
Settlement fees	71
Student credit cards	20
Student loans	42
Tax benefits	81
Tax traps	37, 67
Teaser rates	74
Title insurance	70
Transunion	3, 7, 9, 111
Truth in Lending Act	4, 88
TRW	6, 9, 111
Underwriting fee	70
USA Group	44
Veterans Administration loans (VA)	77
Wasteful daily spendings	49

About The Author

Shaun Aghili is a Certified Financial Planner and a licensed California real estate broker who graduated from the Catholic University of America in Washington, D. C. As a wholesale account executive and a retail loan officer, Shaun is responsible for over 2000 successful loan transactions in the past seven years. Shaun lives in Walnut Creek, CA where his popular monthly "mortgage notes" column appears in several bay area local newspapers.

Are You Ready To Cross The Narrow Gate?

Shaun Aghili's latest book, "Crossing the Narrow Gate," is a delightful personal finance guide in form of an inspiring allegory.

Known as the "no-nonsense financial expert," Aghili maintains that we are "in a world inundated with financial information; but, we are all starving for meaning!" He brings his message of hope and encouragement, along with his vast personal finance knowledge, to thousands every year who want to make sense of the "money" game.

Get the fascinating facts about:

- Why some people never seem to get ahead in life financially.
- How to build a solid financial foundation.
- How the amazing forces of compound interest can make or break you!
- Why your job is much more than a mere paycheck!
- How to start a serious long term investment program with just $100!
- A surefire way to always have a plentiful savings account!
- How to invest in the stock market and not get burned!
- How to open the floodgates of prosperity in your life.
- How our attitudes and deeply rooted beliefs affect our earning power.
- Why most people never reach their true financial potential.
- How to stop accumulating credit card debt starting today!
- What is the most important factor in any consumer loan? (No! it's not the rate!)

And much more!

Order a copy today at *www.thewealthweb.com*

Book order form

Additional copies of this work may be obtained through your favorite book store or by contacting I.L.S. Publishing directly.

Fax orders: (714) 474-0898
Postal orders: I.L.S. Publishing
2222 Michelson Dr. Suite 222-252
Irvine, CA 92616

( ) Please also include a FREE copy of Shaun Aghili's Personal Finance Communique with my order.

Name: _____

Mailing address: _____

City: _____ State: _____ Zip code: _____

Telephone: (____) _____ Work? Home? (Please circle one)

Email address: _____

Sales tax: California Residents, please add 7.75% to your order.
Shipping: $4.00 for the first book. $2.00 for each additional book.

Payment:

    ( ) Check made payable to I.L.S. Publishing

    ( ) Visa

    ( ) Master Card

Card number:

Name on card:

Expiration date:

Book order form

Additional copies of this work may be obtained through your favorite book store or by contacting I.L.S. Publishing directly.

Fax orders: (714) 474-0898
Postal orders: I.L.S. Publishing
2222 Michelson Dr. Suite 222-252
Irvine, CA 92616

( ) Please also include a FREE copy of Shaun Aghili's Personal Finance Communique with my order.

Name: _____

Mailing address: _____

City: _____ State: _____ Zip code: _____

Telephone: (___) _____ Work? Home? (Please circle one)

Email address: _____

Sales tax: California Residents, please add 7.75% to your order.
Shipping: $4.00 for the first book. $2.00 for each additional book.

Payment:

    ( ) Check made payable to I.L.S. Publishing

    ( ) Visa

    ( ) Master Card

Card number:

Name on card:

Expiration date: